Electoral Politics at the Local Level
in the German Federal Republic

University of Florida Monographs
Social Sciences No. 56

Electoral Politics at the Local Level

in the German Federal Republic

Linda L. Dolive

A University of Florida Book

The University Presses of Florida
Gainesville / 1976

Library of Congress Cataloging in Publication Data

Dolive, Linda L.
 Electoral politics at the local level in the German
Federal Republic.

  (University of Florida monographs: Social sciences;
no. 56)
  "A University of Florida book."
  Bibliography: p.
  1. Local elections—Germany, West. 2. Political
parties—Germany, West. I. Title. II. Series:
Florida. University, Gainesville. University of Florida
monographs: Social sciences; no. 56.
JS5459.D64   329'.00943   76–26473
ISBN 0–8130–0554–X

TYPOGRAPHY BY MODERN TYPOGRAPHERS, INCORPORATED
CLEARWATER, FLORIDA

PRINTED BY STORTER PRINTING COMPANY, INCORPORATED
GAINESVILLE, FLORIDA

Acknowledgments

The author wishes to thank David P. Conradt for his encouragement for the undertaking of this study and his valuable advice and criticism throughout. The author also appreciates the helpful comments of Sidney Tarrow and Arnold J. Heidenheimer on an earlier version of the manuscript.

Thanks must also go to the Graduate School of the University of Florida for making possible the publication of this monograph.

Special thanks are due to Henry C. Dolive for his methodological assistance in the analysis of the data, his numerous suggestions and insights for the writing, and above all, his patience and cooperation during the entire process.

Contents

1. Vote-Structuring as a Function of Political Parties   1

2. The German *Gemeinde*   11

3. Electoral Politics at the Local Level   26

4. The Politicization of Local Elections   44

5. Electoral Participation   57

6. National Parties and Their Local Electorates   66

7. The Development of Party Systems   82

8. The Relationship of Parties to Local Electoral Behavior   91

Appendixes   95

Bibliography   103

To
MY MOTHER AND FATHER
and
HENRY and DEVIN

1. Vote-Structuring as a Function of Political Parties

INTRODUCTION

T HE comparative study of political party systems occupies the attention of a large number of political scientists and sociologists.[1] An important premise among such scholars is that political parties are the main vote-structuring agencies in universal mass elections. The student of vote-structuring at the national level in most countries inevitably studies political parties, because they attempt such structuring more continually and comprehensively than do other kinds of agencies.[2] The study of voting and the study of party become almost synonymous. The question then turns to the number of parties participating in the structuring and the division of the vote among them.

The proliferation of studies derived from analyses of voting statistics and sample surveys, made possible by the widespread advent of computer technology, furnished significant descriptions of the voting behavior of mass electorates with their concurrent party preferences. More recently, concern has focused on the ways societal conflicts are translated via the ballot box into various kinds of party systems with an emphasis on the historical dimension of party development.[3]

---

1. Illustrative of such studies are: Joseph LaPalombara and Myron Weiner, eds., *Political Parties and Political Development*; Seymour M. Lipset and Stein Rokkan, eds., *Party Systems and Voter Alignments: Cross-National Perspectives*; Leon Epstein, *Political Parties in Western Democracies*; and Stein Rokkan et al., *Citizens, Elections, Parties.* In this note and subsequent notes, shortened references are given. For full bibliographical information, see Bibliography.

2. See Anthony King, "Political Parties in Western Democracies: Some Sceptical Reflections," p. 121, and Epstein, pp. 77–97.

3. See Lipset and Rokkan, *Party Systems and Voter Alignments.*

THE GERMAN PARTY SYSTEM

The incongruences of German history and their manifestation in the radically different political systems of the present century have made the German party system a subject of intense concern among students of political parties. Article 21 of the Basic Law of the German Federal Republic explicitly recognizes the role of political parties to "participate in forming the political will of the people"; thus, the function of parties as structurers of the vote is formally recognized in the German political process.[4] The pattern of vote-structuring today indicates what has been called the transformation of the German party system—a change from a multi-party system to what is in effect a two-party system, and a change from the predominance of the Christian Democratic Union to an alternation in power between the Christian Democratic Union and the Social Democratic Party. The two trends strengthen the possibility of an institutionalization of democratic structures in Germany.[5]

The movement toward a two-party system is perhaps symptomatic of the weakening of the traditional political and social cleavages inimical to the basically consensual nature of a democracy.[6] The transformation of a multi-party system to a predominantly two-party system is summarized in a review of federal electoral returns (Table 1).[7] The combined strength of the CDU/CSU and the SPD has increased steadily with each election. Of the other parties, the FDP is the only one to have retained a nationwide following.

4. U.S., Department of State, *The Bonn Constitution: Basic Law for the Federal Republic of Germany*, p. 8.

5. "Institutionalization is the process by which organizations and procedures acquire value and stability." Samuel P. Huntington, *Political Order in Changing Societies*, p. 12. For discussions of institutionalization as applied to Germany, see Lewis J. Edinger, "Political Change in Germany," and Werner Kaltefleiter, "The Impact of the Election of 1969 and the Formation of the New Government on the German Party System." The entire issue of *Comparative Politics* in which these articles appear is devoted to an analysis of the German party system.

6. Edinger, p. 568.

7. The electoral system is one of modified proportional representation. Each voter casts two ballots—one for a district deputy and one for a state (*Land*) party list. Since 1953, 50 per cent of the *Bundestag* deputies are elected from the single member districts and 50 per cent from the state lists. A party must average 5 per cent of the national vote or win at least three district contests to secure representation in the *Bundestag*.

The first fatalities in the consolidation of the party system were the small regional parties. The Center Party (ZP) and the German Party (DP), which last won the statutory 5 per cent in 1953 and 1957 elections respectively, survived largely through the aid of the CDU.[8] Other minor parties representing special interest groups disappeared as their constituencies were integrated into the national system.[9]

TABLE 1
PERCENTAGE OF PARTY VOTE RECEIVED BY MAJOR
PARTIES IN FEDERAL ELECTIONS, 1949–72[a]

Year	CDU/CSU	SPD	FDP	Others	CDU/CSU + SPD
1949	31.0	29.2	11.9	23.7	60.2
1953	45.2	28.8	9.5	16.5	74.0
1957	50.2	31.8	7.7	10.3	82.0
1961	45.3	36.2	12.8	5.7	81.5
1965	47.6	39.3	9.5	3.6	86.9
1969	46.1	42.7	5.8	5.4	88.8
1972	44.9	45.8	8.4	0.9	90.7

a. Second ballot returns. The official names of the parties are Christian Democratic Union/Christian Social Union, Social Democratic Party, and Free Democratic Party.

The trend toward a two-party system is reinforced at the state level. Table 2 gives the combined CDU and SPD vote for each state in the first *Landtag* election and in the last *Landtag* election preceding the 1972 federal election.

In terms of *Bundestag* representation, the consolidation of the party system is supported by the vote-seat distribution distorted by the 5 per cent clause.[10] Whereas ten parties won seats in 1949, in 1953 only six parties gained entry into the legislative chamber, and the CDU/CSU gained an absolute majority of the seats. The reduction continued so that in 1957 only four parties crossed the representative barrier. In 1961 the present pattern was completed when the CDU/CSU, SPD, and FDP held all parliamentary seats (Table 3).

8. For example, the German Party won six direct sets in the *Bundestag*. In five of these seats, the party was unopposed by the CDU. Samuel H. Barnes et al., "The German Party System and the 1961 Federal Election," p. 900. See also Uwe K. Kitzinger, *German Electoral Politics*.

9. Illustrative of such special interest parties were the Economic Reconstruction Association (WAV) and the Refugee Party (BHE).

10. For a discussion of the relationship between the electoral law and the party system, see David P. Conradt, "Electoral Law Politics in West Germany."

The pattern of vote division among German parties today thus stands in stark contrast to the multiplicity of voter preferences in the Weimar era, which demonstrated extreme cultural fragmentation and the lack of a supportive consensual basis for democratic politics. The movement toward a two-party system of government and opposition

TABLE 2
Landtag ELECTIONS: PERCENTAGE OF VOTE
RECEIVED BY CDU AND SPD

State	1946–47	1970–72
Bavaria (CSU & SPD)	80.9	89.7
Baden-Wuerttemberg	72.8[a]	90.5
Bremen	63.7	86.9
Hamburg	69.8	88.1
Hesse	73.7	85.6
Lower Saxony	63.3	92.0
North Rhine–Westphalia	69.6	92.4
Rhineland-Palatinate	81.5	90.5
Saar		88.6
Schleswig-Holstein	85.4	92.9

a. Percentage of vote was obtained by averaging the results from the three states of Baden, Wuerttemberg-Baden, and Wuerttemberg-Hohenzollern.

TABLE 3
PERCENTAGE OF *Bundestag* SEATS RECEIVED
BY MAJOR PARTIES, 1949–72

Year	CDU/CSU	SPD	FDP	Others	CDU/CSU + SPD
1949	34.6	32.6	12.9	15.7	67.2
1953	50.1	31.0	9.9	9.0	81.1
1957	54.3	34.0	8.3	3.4	88.3
1961	48.5	38.1	13.4		86.6
1965	49.4	40.7	9.9		90.1
1969	48.8	45.2	6.0		94.0
1972	45.4	46.4	8.3		91.8

on the national and state levels in the German Federal Republic is characteristic of the normal development of regime institutionalization.[11]

In spite of the SPD's growing attractiveness to the voters, until the 1960s the CDU dominated the government under the strong leader-

11. Edinger, p. 572.

ship of Chancellor Adenauer.[12] With his demise and Ludwig Erhard's weak leadership as chancellor and party chairman, the SPD for the first time gained national power through their entry into the Grand Coalition of 1966.[13] Alternation in government between the major parties was finally attained after the 1969 election when the SPD assumed leadership. The 1969 election, whereby a smooth transition of power between major competing parties was achieved (a crucial test of democratic stability), thus symbolizes the substantial political change which has occurred in the transformation of the German party system.[14]

CONCEPTUAL FRAMEWORK

In this discussion, the attention paid to citizens' preferences has been confined so far to national political behavior. From considering a nation as a unit for the purposes of gathering aggregate statistical data, however, a "whole-nation bias" results. Although a political system may be bound together by many nationwide features, it is composed of a variety of political subcommunities. These communities are the environment in which political behavior occurs, and study of an individual's political environment bears directly upon an analysis of his electoral behavior.[15] The socioeconomic and political environments of voters vary considerably intranationally, yet, for the sake of generalization, these dispersions are often simplified into a uniform set of stimuli affecting voter behavior. Such macroanalysis, disregarding the significant within-nation variations in political behavior, is inadequate for the study of the relationship of political parties to voting behavior.

12. For a comprehensive treatment of the topic, see Arnold J. Heidenheimer, *Adenauer and the CDU.*
13. See Linda J. Landers, "The Decline in the Authority and Prestige of Ludwig Erhard as West German Chancellor."
14. The entire issue of *Politische Vierteljahreschrift* 14, no. 2 (June 1973) is devoted to analyses of the German party system. For discussions of the 1969 election, see David P. Conradt, *The West German Party System: An Ecological Analysis of Social Structure and Voting Behavior, 1961–1969*, and Max Kaase, "Determinants of Voting Behavior in the West German General Election of 1969." For analyses of earlier elections, see Erwin K. Scheuch and Rudolf Wildenmann, *Zur Sociologie der Wahl*; Wolfgang Hirsch-Weber and Klaus Schuetz, *Waehler und Gewaehlte*; and Erwin Faul, *Wahlen und Waehler in Westdeutschland*. Faul introduces comparative data from the Weimar and Reich periods in his analysis of postwar electoral behavior.
15. Angus Campbell et al., *The American Voter: An Abridgement*, pp. 145–59.

Studies examining the role of parties intranationally in various countries point out the folly of ignoring the structural contexts of local political behavior. V. O. Key early suggested that general theories about American parties had little relevance to the description of local political behavior.[16] Writing twenty years later, other students of the American party system still concluded that "the data are far from sufficient to permit more than the most speculative generalizations about the nature of the local electorate."[17] In his study of French communities, Mark Kesselman vividly describes the discontinuities in local and national political habits and their reflection in the party system.[18] Students of the Scandinavian party systems advance the most prolific and persuasive arguments for the importance of comparative community analysis through their time series analyses of electoral behavior.[19]

From most countries, however, information about party and voting on the local level is scanty; and Germany is no exception. Despite the interest in and the extensive research on the German party system, the local party system has been ignored. There has been no analysis of local electoral behavior to distinguish the role of political parties at the base of the political system, where the majority of citizens form their attitudes toward the political process. Because the contextual conditioning of electoral behavior is significant, much of the current party research investigates primary and secondary group influence on voters. The variables of class, religion, age, and sex account for much of the variation in national voting behavior in Germany as well as in other countries. Yet the impact of the immediate social and political environment (the community) has been disregarded.[20] The fragility of macrogeneralizations is notable, whether they are made about the functions of political parties or the historical importance of German communities.

16. *Politics, Parties, and Pressure Groups*, p. 224.

17. Robert R. Alford and Eugene C. Lee, "Voting Turnout in American Cities," p. 796. For a recent survey analysis, see Howard D. Hamilton, "The Municipal Voter: Voting and Nonvoting in City Elections."

18. Mark Kesselman, *The Ambiguous Consensus: A Study of Local Government in France.*

19. In addition to the works cited by Rokkan *supra*, see Stein Rokkan, ed., *Approaches to the Study of Political Participation*; Erik Allardt, "Implications of Within-Nation Variations and Regional Imbalances for Cross-National Research"; Stein Rokkan and Henry Valen, "Regional Contrasts in Norwegian Politics"; and Stein Rokkan, "Electoral Mobilization, Party Competition, and National Integration."

20. Cf. Kesselman and Hamilton.

The individual's voting behavior is affected by both the range of alternatives available and the alignment of the forces conditioning it, and these are not the same in all elections.[21] In the United States, for example, an individual's voting pattern in local elections (which are largely nonpartisan) will be different from his voting pattern in partisan national elections. On the local level, in almost two-thirds of American municipalities of 5,000 or more inhabitants, parties do not perform the primary function of vote-structuring.[22]

The absence or weakness of national political parties in local elections is a noteworthy attribute of local politics in several European countries as well. Small-town French local elections are distinguished by their lack of competitive party lists. Of particular interest is the extremely weak local position of the Gaullist party. It obtained 41 per cent of the deputy seats in the 1967 national elections, compared to a mere 9 per cent of the municipal council seats in the 1965 local elections.[23] In Norwegian local elections, nonpartisan lists appeared on approximately two-fifths of local electoral ballots in 1963.[24] The dominant national party, the Labor Party, contests most but not all local elections, but the nonsocialist parties are much less likely to enter local contests.[25] In Belgian local elections, except in large cities, the vote contenders are not the national parties but instead a large number of local groups which run under a variety of names such as "Impartial," "Friends of the People," and "One against All."[26] In Switzerland, one-half of the twenty-four communes under a proportional representational electoral system have at least one purely communal group in local elections in addition to national parties.[27] The most striking contrast between electoral levels is in the lesser number

21. Stein Rokkan, "Citizen Participation in Political Life: A Comparison of Data for Norway and the United States of America," p. 365.
22. Willis D. Hawley, *Nonpartisan Elections and the Case for Party Politics*, p. 16. Some examples of the discussion of nonpartisanship in the American setting include: Charles R. Adrian, "Some Characteristics of Nonpartisan Elections"; Fred I. Greenstein, *The American Party System and the American People*, pp. 66–70; and Phillips Cutright, "Nonpartisan Electoral Systems in American Cities."
23. Kesselman, p. 1010.
24. Rokkan, "Electoral Mobilization," p. 251.
25. Henry Valen, "Norway: The 1967 Local Elections," p. 238.
26. Stephen Holt, *Six European States*, p. 299.
27. George Codding, Jr., *Governing the Commune of Veyrier: Politics in Swiss Local Government*, p. 31.

of active parties at the communal level.[28] Other differences between Swiss national and local elections are manifested in the weakness of important national parties locally, and, likewise, the local strength of declining national parties.

Also in Germany on the local level, vote-structuring often takes place without any parties at all or with parties as only one of many contending forces.[29] In the states of Rhineland-Palatinate, Hesse, Bavaria, Baden-Wuerttemberg, and Lower Saxony, the nonpartisan character of local elections is particularly apparent. Many elections are not contested by groups at all, and in others local voter groups monopolize the ballot. For example, in the 1972 Hessian local elections almost one-third of the council seats were won by non–party affiliated councilors.[30] In the 1968 Lower Saxony elections, local voter groups obtained one-quarter of the local electoral vote.[31] In Bavaria, local voter groups have obtained one-half of the local vote.[32] In Baden-Wuerttemberg in the late 1960s, of 3,300 municipalities, 3,000 had non–party affiliated elected mayors.[33] In Rhineland-Palatinate local elections in 1969, nonpartisan candidates obtained two-fifths of the municipal council seats.[34]

An examination of voting behavior at the local level in several countries indicates that political parties do not necessarily live up to their analysts' notions of the functions they perform, and the number of critical evaluations of the state of knowledge about parties grows.[35]

Neglect of the study of local elections assumes an extra dimension in the case of German political parties. Postwar governmental recon-

28. Ibid., pp. 25–26; and Urs Jaeggi, *Berggemeinden im Wandel*, pp. 75–77.

29. Heino Kaack, *Geschichte und Struktur des deutschen Parteiensystems*, pp. 475–76.

30. Hesse, *Beitraege zur Statistik Hessens*, nr. 54, *Die Kommunalwahlen am 22. Oktober 1972*, p. 7.

31. Lower Saxony, *Statistik von Niedersachsen, Band 118, Die Kommunalwahlen in Niedersachsen am 29. September 1968*, Part 1, p. 15.

32. Bavaria, *Beitraege zur Statistik Bayerns, Heft 220, Kommunalwahlen in Bayern am 27. Maerz 1960*, pp. 51–53.

33. Theodor Pfizer, *Kommunalpolitik*, p. 39.

34. Rhineland-Palatinate, *Statistik von Rheinland-Pfalz, Band 195, Die Kommunalwahlen in Rheinland-Pfalz am 8. Juni 1969*, p. 13.

35. See Howard A. Scarrow, "The Function of Political Parties: A Critique of the Literature and the Approach"; King, pp. 111–41; Theodore Lowi, "Toward Functionalism in Political Science: The Case of Innovation in Party Systems"; Giovanni Sartori, "From the Sociology of Politics to Political Sociology"; and Peter H. Merkl, "Political Cleavages and Party Systems."

struction gave initial and special emphasis to the municipal level of government.[36] Political parties were first formed at the municipal (*Gemeinde*) level, with the result that local elections were held in 1946, three years before the first federal election. The restoration of democracy at the grass-roots or *Gemeinde* level was a basic objective of the Potsdam Agreement: "The administration of affairs in Germany should be directed toward the decentralization of the political structure and the development of local responsibility . . . (i) local self-government shall be restored throughout Germany on democratic principles and in particular through elective councils as rapidly as consistent with military security and the purposes of military occupation; (ii) all democratic political parties with rights of assembly and of public discussions shall be allowed and encouraged throughout Germany; (iii) representative and elective principles shall be introduced into regional, provincial, and state (*Land*) administration as rapidly as may be justified by the successful application of these principles in local self-government."[37]

The importance of these initial party formations and electoral competition at the local level in conditioning the subsequent development of the party system has been discussed but not validated through any time series analysis.[38] No investigation has been attempted for the purpose of finding out if and how political parties did, in effect, gain the initiative in local politics.

A research orientation toward municipalities and political parties at the municipal level has an additional asset as an approach to the study of party systems and voting behavior. The *Gemeinde* is a data unit with which people identify themselves and others. Other units such as voting districts and precincts are purely administrative. By choosing an area which corresponds to citizens' awareness and identity, the researcher may make his interpretation of ecological data more acceptable and comprehensible.[39] The *Gemeinde* as a foundation of collective life has a double function. For the individual, the *Gemeinde* is the home and social room in which he lives. For the society, the *Ge-*

36. See Edward H. Litchfield and Associates, *Governing Postwar Germany.*
37. "Report of the Tripartite Conference of Berlin," quoted in Herbert Jacob, *German Administration since Bismarck: Central Authority versus Local Autonomy,* p. 154.
38. Gerhard Loewenberg, "The Remaking of the German Party System: Political and Socioeconomic Factors."
39. Allardt, p. 340.

meinde is part of a whole and is tied in with social, political, and cultural attributes. Because the *Gemeinde* is "a relatively closed whole and at the same time only a part," it has unique status as an object of study.[40]

In examining the relationship of political parties to local electoral behavior in Germany, the writer of this study focuses upon three categories of information: the characteristics of local electoral politics (e.g., the pattern of voters' preferences toward vote-structuring entities, the incidence of national political parties, and the degree of electoral participation); the relationship of ecological and political variables in local voting behavior (e.g., the social and economic conditions that influence voter support for specific entities, especially those conditions associated with the initial formation and subsequent maintenance of political parties); and the tie-in between the behavior of local electorates and that of national and state electorates (e.g., characteristics of voters at the various levels of electoral politics, and the effect of the local party-vote relationship on the national party-vote relationship and vice versa). The background against which the behavior of local electorates must be considered is the *Gemeinde*.

---

40. Renate Mayntz, *Soziale Schichtung und Sozialer Wandel in einer Industriegemeinde*, p. 1.

2. The German *Gemeinde*

THE term "local government" may be applied in two ways, referring either to government by local agents appointed by and responsible to the central government, or to government by freely elected local bodies, enabled with power and responsibility in certain respects, and although subject to the supremacy of a national government, exercising control over local concerns.[1] German communities have tended to the tradition of communal autonomy.[2]

Many *Gemeinden* have a long history of independence, preceding the foundation of the nation-state. The autonomy of cities was characteristic of the twelfth and thirteenth centuries. As monarchical rule developed and consolidation occurred, especially in Prussia, the medieval political power of the communities declined. However, local self-government, as an important part of German politics, was revived in the nineteenth century following Napoleon's defeat of Prussia. The man most associated with this resurrection was the Baron von Stein, the chief architect of the municipal ordinance act of 1808.[3] The reforms established a system of municipal self-government with local citizen participation. Stein's belief that local self-government was the foundation of a free state influenced communal development until 1933.

The Weimar Constitution explicitly recognized this current of thought in democratizing the legal foundations of local government. Article 127 stated: "*Gemeinde* and *Gemeindeverbaende* have the right of self-government within the limits of the laws."[4] In place of the Prus-

---

1. G. Montagu Harris, *Comparative Local Government*, p. 9.
2. For a comprehensive survey of the historical development of German local government, see Erich Becker, "Entwicklung der deutschen Gemeinden und Gemeindeverbaende im Hinblick auf die Gegenwart."
3. See Ernst Utzinger, *Die freie politische Gemeinde in der Schweiz und im Ausland*, pp. 54–60. See also Becker, pp. 77–83.
4. Becker, pp. 100–101.

sian system of three-class suffrage, selection of representative bodies at all levels of government was made by universal, equal, direct, and secret suffrage through a proportional representation (PR) electoral system. State constitutions also reflected the right to popularly elected municipal councils. Although the forms of local self-government varied among the states, three types were characteristic. A single council system, which combined legislative and executive functions, was dominant in South Germany. An elected council, which then chose the mayor with long tenure who held the executive functions, was characteristic of the Rhineland section; Konrad Adenauer, the mayor of Cologne from 1917 to 1933, typified this "dominant mayor" form. A bicameral municipal legislature was common in the Prussian areas of North Germany. The lower house, elected directly by the people, invested executive power in a plural board of magistrates which served as the upper chamber.[5]

Autonomy as a cornerstone of municipal government was completely discarded during the Nazi period. The German Municipal Government Act of 1935 abolished all local elections. Mayors and city councilors were agents of the Nazi party and national government and were appointed by these upper levels.

The historical tradition of local self-government was resumed in the postwar period. As early as 1942, allied officials planned for a grassroots approach to reconstruction through local self-government.[6] The desire to return to the pre-Hitler forms was expressly stated in the Potsdam Agreement. The initiation of German reconstruction at the local level was made more necessary in that no higher levels of government remained. While the boundaries of most German states were substantially altered by the allied powers, the *Gemeinde* remained relatively intact. The heritage of self-government of many communities was thus preserved and strengthened. Local *Gemeinde* organizations and elections were authorized in the occupied zones between 1945 and 1946.

Local self-government as an institution is protected in Article 28 of the Basic Law of 1949: " 'Gemeinde' must be guaranteed the right to regulate, under their own responsibility and within the limits of the

    5. See Arnold J. Heidenheimer, *The Governments of Germany*, p. 203. See also Litchfield and Associates, p. 60.
    6. Litchfield and Associates, p. 58.

laws, all the affairs of the local community."[7] Various articles in the state constitutions further reinforce the right of the *Gemeinde* to self-government.[8] Legally, local governments have the right to perform tasks not expressly prohibited or otherwise regulated by laws—in contrast to other systems of local government whereby the units may perform only those tasks prescribed in their charters or by national and state laws.[9]

THE STRUCTURE OF LOCAL GOVERNMENT

The basic units of the political system range in area and population from the village of fewer than one hundred inhabitants to the metropolis of more than one million. The structure of the municipalities is being altered through local government reorganization acts passed by the state legislatures. Recognizing the inability of many small towns to perform the tasks of local government in the modern world, the states are decreasing the number of *Gemeinden*. Through consolidation and dissolution, the number of municipalities has decreased from 24,282 in 1968 to 15,857 in 1973.[10] The anticipated minimum size of a *Gemeinde* varies from state to state, but in general, according to the reorganization acts, the ideal *Gemeinde* envisaged will contain at least five thousand inhabitants. In spite of the reorganizations, the overwhelming majority of municipalities are small. Ninety-eight per cent have populations of fewer than twenty thousand, and 47.4 per cent of the German population lives in these small cities or villages.[11]

In every *Gemeinde* is an elected council, the main representative body of the community. The councils range in size from five to eighty members, with the number of councilors set by state laws according to the population of the municipality. Local elections in most states occur every four years. Within a state, all local elections occur on the same day, the election date varying from state to state. In Bavaria and

---

7. Roger H. Wells, *The States in West German Federalism*, p. 75.
8. Appendix A contains excerpted articles from the Constitution of Rhineland-Palatinate that pertain to the rights of local self-government.
9. A legal discussion of the relationship of the *Gemeinde* to the national government is presented in Arnold Koettgen, *Die Gemeinde und der Bundesgesetzgeber*.
10. Hans Ulrich Behn, *Die Bundesrepublik Deutschland*, p. 25.
11. Germany, Statistisches Bundesamt, *Statistisches Jahrbuch fuer die Bundesrepublik Deutschland, 1973*, p. 44.

Baden-Wuerttemberg, local office tenure is six years, with half of the council elected every three years.[12] The method of election varies among the states but two forms are common: plurality elections and proportional representational elections. Many states adopt a "closed list" system whereby the voter must choose among lists rather than individual candidates. If, however, only one list or no list for the municipal council is submitted, a plurality election is permitted. Each voter can then cast ballots for as many council members as are to be elected. He may vote for the candidates on the ballot, or he may write in names. The persons with most votes are elected. No label indicating political affiliation appears on the ballot. If two or more lists are submitted, a proportional representational election results. The voter casts his ballot for one list. Seats are distributed among those lists obtaining at least 5 per cent of the vote by the d'Hondt method of allocation.

A second important feature of municipal election codes relates to the right of local voter groups that are not political parties in the sense of Article 21 (as interpreted by the Federal Constitutional Court) to submit lists. The Saar, for instance, excluded local voter groups and individual candidates by adopting a municipal electoral law whereby only parties in the sense of Article 21 could submit lists. However, in July 1960, the Federal Constitutional Court reversed this law, ruling that denial of the right of nomination to candidates other than those of political parties violated the principle of equal opportunity and the guarantees of local self-government.[13] Consequently, nonparty groups have legal recognition of their right to candidate nomination in the local election laws of the states.

The organizational structures of the *Gemeinde* are determined by state law and reflect regional diversity and modified organizational forms of the Weimar period.[14] These structures are uniform within a state. The states of North Rhine–Westphalia, Lower Saxony, and Hesse center administrative powers in a nonpolitical city manager who is responsible to the elected city council.[15] Local governments in

12. Appendix B presents a summary of local election laws, by states. See also Ruediger R. Beer, *Die Gemeinde*, pp. 71–74.
13. Arthur B. Gunlicks, "Representative and Party at the Local Level in Western Germany: The Case of Lower Saxony," p. 91.
14. See Arnold Koettgen, "Wesen und Rechtsform der Gemeinden und Gemeindeverbaende."
15. In towns of fewer than 100 inhabitants in Hesse and Lower Saxony, a *Gemeindeversammlung* (town meeting) replaces the elected communal council.

Schleswig-Holstein exhibit a similar form, with a collegial executive. Rhineland-Palatinate continues in its tradition of a "dominant mayor" system, with the mayor responsible to the council. The elected municipal council combines executive and legislative functions in the states of Bavaria and Baden-Wuerttemberg, and the mayor is directly elected by the citizens. The city states of Bremen and Hamburg combine the functions of municipal and state governments in a collegial executive, the senate.[16]

The tasks of local government include technical concerns such as regulation of utilities and operation of public transportation; maintenance of cultural institutions, including schools, libraries, theaters, and museums: social welfare work such as the administration of hospitals, health care services, homes for the aged, and public welfare assistance; and communal tasks such as street maintenance and city planning.[17] Local governments are empowered to obtain revenue for carrying out their responsibilities through two forms of taxes (*Realsteuern*). The most important local tax source is the *Gewerbesteuer*, which is levied on the production and capital investment of industrial and commercial enterprises. The other tax (*Grundsteuer*) derives from real estate holdings. Communities may also levy local taxes on such items as beverages, entertainment, and hunting licenses.[18]

As the scope of activities and services increases in an industrialized society, local governments, while not without their own sources of revenue, are increasingly dependent upon higher levels of government for financial support. Funds from the state treasuries supplement the funds the local governments can obtain on their own and to some extent equalize the financial strength of cities. Cities with a large industrial base are in a better financial situation than others—although financing remains a major problem for local governments.[19] The German

16. See Heidenheimer, *The Governments of Germany*, p. 204, and Koettgen, "Wesen und Rechtsform der Gemeinden," pp. 199–205.

17. Thomas Ellwein, *Das Regierungssystem der Bundesrepublik Deutschland*, p. 40. See also Hans Peters, ed., *Handbuch der kommunalen Wissenschaft und Praxis*, vol. 2, *Kommunale Verwaltung*.

18. Rhineland-Palatinate, *Statistik von Rhineland-Pfalz, Band 111, Gemeindestatistik Rheinland-Pfalz 1960/1961, Teil V, Gemeindefinanzen*, p. 11.

19. The average city depends on state subsidies for approximately 20 per cent of its budget. The financial position of cities was strengthened in the Finance Reform of 1969 whereby cities may claim specified amounts of certain state income and business taxes. Heidenheimer, *The Governments of Germany*, pp. 199, 205.

tradition of local self-government does not, however, equate financial dependence or administrative interdependence with a lack of communal autonomy. Self-government is viewed almost exclusively in terms of autonomy in the execution of local tasks and in the independence of decisions reached by freely elected governmental organs.[20]

To perform the services which are beyond the means of individual municipalities, both administratively and financially, most *Gemeinden* are joined in *Gemeindeverbaende* (associations.) The most basic and common type is the *Kreis* (county). The more populous cities obtain the legal distinction of *Stadtkreis* (city-county); there are no uniform rules as to when a *Gemeinde* obtains *Stadtkreis* status.[21] The primary organs of county government are an elected council (*Kreistag*) and an executive official, the *Landrat*, who is elected by the council, except in Bavaria, where he is elected directly by the people. In several states, an intervening joint authority is created between the *Gemeinde* and the *Kreis*: the *Amt*, which unites several small neighboring communities for administrative purposes. Additional intermunicipal associations (*Zweckverbaende*) are created for specific purposes such as maintenance of utilities. There are 5,000 such special authorities in Germany.[22]

The counties, in addition to performing joint operations that their member communities are incapable of, serve to redistribute taxes for local purposes. Counties, like municipalities, depend upon state treasuries. State grants-in-aid account for an average of one-half of the counties' revenues, although such reliance varies greatly from state to state. For instance, in Bavaria state grants total 63.9 per cent of the counties' incomes, but counties in North Rhine–Westphalia derive only 37.9 per cent of their income from the state.[23]

A discussion of a *Gemeinde* in terms of its institutional structures and its financial and administrative reliance upon the state gives by no means a complete portrayal. A *Gemeinde*, as a community, may have an extensive social and political influence upon its inhabitants. In spite of the mobility inherent in modern society, the majority of the people spend a large part, if not all, of their lives in a single com-

---

20. Gunlicks, "Representative and Party," p. 105.
21. Only 110 of the *Gemeinden* had *Stadtkreis* status in 1973. Behn, p. 28.
22. Wells, p. 76.
23. Jacob, p. 189.

munity. The *Gemeinde*, then, signifies an important dimension of a total life experience; it is the foundation and common denominator of a variety of social activities.[24] Local influences stemming from a distinct sociocultural environment leave their imprint on the political process.

THE STYLE OF LOCAL POLITICS

In studying local government, when we turn from the legalistic and administrative aspects and consider local politics, we find little systematized knowledge. This section of our discussion, based upon the meager amount of information on politics at the *Gemeinde* level in Germany and supplemented by studies of local politics in other countries, is an attempt to illuminate local political habits, providing a background against which to set the extensive electoral analyses in the following chapters.

The prime characteristics of *Gemeinden* are their large number and their small size; thus, when we speak of local government we mean predominantly that of the smaller cities, towns, and villages. If we apply the formal criteria of size of community and density of population to distinguish between rural and urban, most *Gemeinden* would be classified as rural.[25] Although these local units are increasingly exposed to outside influences, the significance of their structure and processes stems partly from the slowness with which local habits change. "Great resistance to change is undoubtedly one factor that makes for the high degree of similarity to be found in the local governmental activity and organization in various countries, in different sections of the same country, and in the same area at different times."[26] In this context, the political importance of the *Gemeinde* lies in its being the only level of government at which most people personally know the leaders and come in direct contact with the political institutions. The impact of local government is both tangible and immediate.

24. Rene Koenig, "Die Gemeinde im Blickfeld der Soziologie," p. 50.

25. Discussion of the significance of the terms *rural* and *urban* are presented in Richard Dewey, "The Rural-Urban Continuum: Real but Relatively Unimportant," and T. Lynn Smith and Paul E. Zopf, Jr., *Principles of Inductive Rural Sociology*, pp. 8–35. For a discussion of German rural-urban cultural differences, see Franz Urban Pappi, *Wahlverhalten und Politische Kultur*, pp. 89–127.

26. Smith and Zopf, pp. 367–68.

This local environment produces citizens who are better informed about local politics and political organizations than national. One study revealed that three-fifths of German respondents were "informed" to some degree about local political organizations, but three-fifths of the same respondents could give no information at all about national political organizations.[27] The level of knowledge about local political leaders is also high. One survey showed that 84 per cent of the respondents knew the mayor and 55 per cent knew other council members as well. Indeed, one-third of the local citizens were able to name three or more council members.[28] Moreover, this survey was conducted in a city with a relatively large proportion of new residents and a mayor who had been in office for a very short time.

Political efficacy is also greater in government at the local level. In Germany as in many other countries, people feel themselves better able to influence policy-making locally than nationally. Sixty-two per cent of the respondents in a nation-wide sample of Germans expressed a belief that they could exert an influence on local government; only 38 per cent felt that they could exert a similar influence on government at the national level.[29] The powerlessness felt by many individuals with regard to their impact on national government does not enter into their feelings about local government. Since individuals know the local leaders and institutions, they perceive problems as more comprehensible and defined, they hold opinions about what should be done, and they have some idea of ways to exert influence.

The accessibility of local officials and the intimacy of personal relationships in *Gemeinde* life are clearly revealed in a consideration of the strategies of influence utilized by local citizens. In both the Almond and Verba and the Pflaum studies, the respondents most often indicated their most effective political resource to be direct contact with local officials: 46 per cent and 52.8 per cent in the respective studies.[30]

Political parties as mediating structures between the individual and his government in the local political process were overwhelmingly rejected. Only 3 per cent of the Almond and Verba sample said they would "work through a political party" in an attempt to influence local

27. Renate Pflaum, "Politische Fuehrung und politische Beteiligung als Ausdruck gemeindlicher Selbstgestaltung," p. 260.
28. Martin Schwonke and Ulfert Herlyn, *Wolfsburg*, p. 146.
29. Gabriel Almond and Sidney Verba, *The Civic Culture*, pp. 142–43.
30. Ibid., p. 158; Pflaum, p. 261.

government; in the Pflaum study the corresponding figure was 6 per cent.[31] These percentages, incidentally, are higher than those for other countries. Fewer than 1 per cent of respondents in the United States, Great Britain, and Italy said that they would work through parties locally to exert influence. Whatever their importance on the national level, political parties on the local level are often bypassed as channels of influence.

Since parties are seldom mentioned by local citizens as a means of influencing local policy-making, it is not surprising that parties are not seen as initiators of that policy-making, either.[32] The local council is viewed far more in terms of individual power holders than in terms of party governors. The public opinion poll results presented in Table 4

TABLE 4
PERCEPTION OF LOCUS OF LOCAL POWER BY SEX
(in percentages)

Greatest Influence over *Gemeinde* Concerns Is Held by:	Men	Women
The *Gemeinde* council	47.2	34.6
The *Gemeinde* director	27.0	23.1
The mayor	5.6	14.1
The political parties (*Fraktionen*)	11.2	2.6
No opinion	9.0	25.6
	N = 89	N = 78

SOURCE: Pflaum, p. 262.

illustrate the weak power position of political parties in *Gemeinde* politics.[33]

The impotence of political parties may be related to the importance of communal personal relationships. A crucial difference in the style of local and national politics derives from the difference between formal and informal group memberships. In the *Gemeinde*, informal groups collect around local notables. People perceive certain individuals to be, by virtue of family background or job, the natural leaders

31. Ibid.
32. Pflaum, pp. 261, 275. See also Mayntz, p. 251.
33. Findings about the low influence profile of the mayor are in contrast to findings about the influence of the mayor in French and Swiss local politics. See Kesselman, pp. 38–52, and Jaeggi, p. 225.

or social actives of the community. The advice and help of these notables is sought by their neighbors in a wide variety of communal activities. As a consequence, political leadership is not specialized, and political recruitment is determined upon the basis of personal characteristics. Some of the more important attributes named by local voters include "Christian ethics, helpfulness, diligence, sense of duty, good family background."[34]

In the sense that voters select local leaders primarily on grounds of their character and personality, parties are not vehicles for leadership. Supportive data for this proposition derives from field research in Switzerland and France. Urs Jaeggi in his study of Swiss communes concluded that electoral candidates were not evaluated in terms of party affiliation. The most important campaign attributes were, instead, personal connections and general standing in the community.[35] Likewise, George Codding found that a candidate's name was his greatest political asset in Swiss municipal elections. Many council members carried the names of the older families in the community and were generally reelected for a number of successive terms in office.[36]

The personal flavor of French local campaigns is also pervasive. Interviews with small-town mayors revealed that one criterion used in the selection of a candidate was the size of his family, the assumption being that the larger a man's family, the greater the number of votes he would win.[37] In sum, an important part in cross-national local elections is played by old family ties, which lead to informal authority in communal affairs. Leadership in a political institution, the municipal council, is one manifestation of a diffused social authority. Table 5 indicates the importance of personal attributes in the selection of local officeholders in Germany.

The significance of a candidate's personality and the insignificance of his party label as influences on local voting behavior are confirmed by a number of other German surveys.[38] Numerous surveys of federal

34. Pflaum, p. 267. See also Benita Luckmann, *Politik in einer deutschen Kleinstadt*, pp. 137–38, 196–98, and Pappi, *Wahlverhalten und Politische Kultur*, p. 98.

35. Jaeggi, p. 73.

36. Codding, pp. 40–41.

37. Sidney Tarrow, "The Urban-Rural Cleavage in Political Involvement: The Case of France," p. 356.

38. See Luckmann, pp. 137, 196–98; Kaack, pp. 475–76; Herbert Koetter, *Struktur and Funktion von Landgemeinden im Einflussbereich einer deutschen*

elections demonstrate, in stark contrast, that very few electors cast their ballots on the basis of a candidate's personality. Survey data of the 1969 federal election campaign show that 62 per cent of the electorate believed they should decide on the basis of "party slates of capable leaders," compared to the 27 per cent who believed they should decide on the basis of "Chancellor candidates."[39]

Another method of evaluating the importance of a party label in federal elections is the analysis of first and second ballots. In 1969, 93.9 per cent of the voters who cast their second ballot (party list)

TABLE 5
DETERMINANTS OF LOCAL VOTE BY SEX
(in percentages)

Deciding Factors in Determining My Vote Were:	Men	Women
Party label	16.3	11.1
Christian ethics	3.3	4.4
Because knew candidate personally	27.2	14.4
Because he is a "good man"	25.0	13.3
Local interests	10.9	4.4
Standes- and personal interests	9.8	4.4
Nonvoters	39.1	58.9
	N = 96	N = 86
	multiple answers permitted	

SOURCE: Pflaum, p. 265.

for the CDU had voted for their CDU district candidate on the first ballot. The corresponding percentage of like SPD ballots was 94.7. Of CDU and SPD second ballots cast in 1965, 93.4 per cent were identical to the party affiliation of the recipient of the first ballot. A very high percentage of voters thus cast both ballots for the same party.[40]

The integrating functions of well-organized, technically efficient political parties in mass society are not as relevant to local electorates.

Mittelstadt, p. 146; Otto Ziebill, *Politische Parteien und kommunale Selbstverwaltung*, p. 58; and Werner Roth, *Dorf im Wandel*, p. 224.

39. Heidenheimer, *The Governments of Germany*, pp. 131–32. Cf. Luckmann, p. 200.

40. For the percentage of like ballots in the 1957 and 1961 elections, see Rodney Stiefbold, "The Significance of Void Ballots in West German Elections," p. 398. For comparative 1953 percentages, see Hirsch-Weber and Schuetz, p. 314.

Personal contact between local leaders and followers makes such integration unnecessary. Eighty per cent of local voters knew personally the candidate for whom they voted.[41] In federal elections, on the other hand, a majority of voters did not know even the name of their district candidate. A national survey conducted in the same period as the local survey cited above demonstrates the lack of familiarity of voters with candidates: only 36 per cent of the voters who had already decided for a party in the 1953 election campaign correctly named their party's candidate; of the undecided voters, only 21 per cent correctly identified *any* candidate by name.[42]

The personality factor combines with other *Gemeinde* norms to diminish the importance of local branches of national political parties. There exists a widespread belief that local government should be nonpolitical or nonpartisan.[43] Political parties are often viewed as foreign bodies intruding upon the political will of the *Gemeinde*. When asked why they shy away from political parties, respondents give answers indicating distrust. "The parties have brought nothing but strife, war, and destruction to Germany."[44] "I cannot foresee what good can come of parties."[45] Thus, party organizations on the local level are viewed as superfluous or worse. Efforts to recruit new party members are in general rebuffed, and party meetings are viewed as propaganda techniques.[46]

To combat these trends the political parties strive to conform to local norms. Party election lists are often composed of nonparty members. Many party candidates stress their independence and their willingness to work for an unpartisan *Gemeinde* will. The propensity of candidates to stress their interest in the communal good and their freedom from party dictates is documented in Swiss local politics as well.[47] Correspondingly, many national parties in Norway show little

---

41. Pflaum, p. 265.

42. Hirsch-Weber and Schuetz, p. 300.

43. See Gunlicks, "Representative and Party," pp. 18–22, 124–26; Pflaum, pp. 256–57, 265; and Werner Grundmann, *Die Rathausparteien*, pp. 92–94.

44. Arthur B. Gunlicks, "Intraparty Democracy in Western Germany," pp. 235–36.

45. Pflaum, p. 258. This belief in the negative worth of political parties is not confined solely to the level of local government. See Wolfgang Hartenstein and Klaus Liepelt, "Party Members and Party Voters in West Germany," p. 44; and Lewis J. Edinger, *Politics in Germany*, pp. 98–100, 284–85.

46. See Pflaum, pp. 257–58, and Gunlicks, "Intraparty Democracy," pp. 235–36.

47. Codding, pp. 28–32, and Jaeggi, p. 77.

interest in emphasizing partisan differences on the communal level.[48] Because of the tendency to vote for the man, sometimes in spite of his party label, German parties compete with each other to secure local notables to be on their election lists. Voters quite often state that a candidate would obtain an equal or better showing on an opposite party list, that the character or personality of the candidate, not the party, is the decisive factor.[49]

Political party groups in the German *Gemeinden* as in other European communes direct their functions primarily toward local affairs.[50] With the exception of the SPD, most local parties have weak connections with higher party organizations.[51] The individuality of the parties' representatives as candidates and councilors remains dominant.

Resistance to partisan local government is supported by physical and attitudinal factors. The small size of *Gemeinden* enables personal relationships to remain determinants of political relationships. A long tradition of local autonomy reinforces the tendency to view political parties as foreign intruders. Thus, the adoption of a party label by a local notable is not necessarily a passport to political office.

Competing alongside the political parties to secure candidates and voters are numerous local voter groups. Many of these groups are formed to compete in only one election and are characteristic of the small towns in which personal relationships are predominant. Loosely organized, such local voter groups disband after the election. There are also permanent local voter group organizations, known as *Rathaus* parties, which, while they have programs and compete in successive elections, shun national party labels.

Personal considerations are a primary factor in the formation of local voter groups. New voter groups often arise when influential municipal figures are dissatisfied either with the incumbents in local office or with their own electoral list positions in their group or party.[52]

48. Stein Rokkan and Henry Valen, "The Mobilization of the Periphery: Data on Turnout, Party Membership and Candidate Recruitment in Norway," p. 192.
49. See Grundmann, p. 9; Pflaum, pp. 266–67, 271; Luckmann, pp. 138, 198; Pfizer, pp. 39–40; and Koetter, p. 146.
50. National parties emphasize local concerns and deemphasize party differences in Swiss local electoral campaigns. Codding, p. 23. For Germany, see Vera Gemmecke, *Parteien im Wahlkampf*, p. 63.
51. See Pflaum, p. 278, and Gunlicks, "Representative and Party," p. 238. For the same tendency in Norway, see Rokkan and Valen, "The Mobilization of the Periphery," p. 197.
52. See Gemmecke, pp. 63–64; Roth, pp. 227–28; and Ziebill, p. 57.

Local electoral codes, which embody a closed list proportional representational system, also cause the formation of local voter groups. Groups of local notables who do not wish a partisan affiliation bind together for tactical reasons. Another predominant type of local voter group is formed by adherents of minor or forbidden political parties. For instance, former Nazis composed local voter groups in the immediate postwar period; after the abolishment of the Communist Party in 1956, its adherents, likewise, often formed local voter groups to enable the contesting of local offices.[53] Other local voter groups are composed to seek representation of the interests of specific economic or social groups, such as the refugees and the war-injured. Finally, there is a body of local voter groups concerned with preserving local amenities.[54]

Local voter groups adopt names such as the Citizens' Union, the Free Voter Association, and the Independent Voter Group of ———, to reflect the desire to be "above" parties.[55] Local voter groups are so strong in some states that the nationally organized political parties are forced to form a coalition to oppose them in local elections.[56] In other locales, the electoral position of the parties is directly dependent upon whether a local voter group decides to compete against them. The CDU and SPD often obtain twice as many votes in a state election as they do within the same voting district in a local election when local voter groups are present.[57] Thus, although some local voter groups have implicit ties or form silent coalitions with national political parties, local voter groups are a distinct phenomenon separate from party organizations and often competitors to parties. The existence of local voter groups reflects an environment where national parties are not desired and yet for one reason or another some group organization may be necessary.

The distinct style of local politics derives in large part from a synthesis of community norms with modern structures. A personalistic basis of politics, combined with universal suffrage, leads to the two local political phenomena of plurality elections and local voter groups. The choices available to the local voter vary tremendously according

53. Vera Ruediger, *Die kommunalen Wahlvereinigungen in Hessen*, pp. 76–84, presents a classification of various types of local voter groups.
54. Grundmann, pp. 8–9.
55. Ibid., pp. 17–19.
56. Ibid., pp. 2–3.
57. See Roth, p. 224, and Gemmecke, p. 63.

to the *Gemeinde* in which he lives. He may choose among individual candidates, among local voter groups, among local voter groups and political parties, or among political parties entirely. Even list alternatives of the political parties will be dissimilar among communities since no party runs in every *Gemeinde*. The alignment of forces influencing voting varies, in other words, not only with the level of government but within each level as well.

In the next chapter, the structured contexts of local electoral behavior will be analyzed in more quantitative terms. The focus will be the difference in voter alternatives between the levels of government. In successive chapters, the variations among *Gemeinden* in rates and directions of electoral change with special reference to the party system will be discussed.

3. Electoral Politics at the Local Level

IN THE preceding chapters, those aspects of the German political system and culture most directly related to electoral politics at the local level of government were considered. The major characteristics of the two foci of this study, the party system and the *Gemeinde*, were presented. However, to assess in depth how votes are structured at the local level, an investigator needs longitudinal and cross-sectional analyses of municipal elections.

Undertaking such analyses, the collector of local electoral statistics encounters many difficulties in preparing the raw data for processing and analysis. Local statistics are not nationally centralized but published by the states individually. Comparison is hindered by the lack of uniformity in the reporting of statistics. States often do not report similar statistics through successive elections; some states publish electoral results only for municipalities over a certain size; and some states provide no summary statistics. The data collection must, therefore, be founded on analysis of local returns from each *Gemeinde* under study.

The accumulation of comparable electoral and demographic statistics was made possible only by the restriction of the data collection to one state, Rhineland-Palatinate. With the *Gemeinde* as the data unit, demographic variables were obtained from the eighteen local, state, and national elections held between 1947 and 1969, and from the 1961 census. A 20 per cent sample of 588 *Gemeinden*, derived according to systematic sampling procedures, is the basis for further analyses utilizing a variety of bi- and multivariate statistical techniques, beginning in chapter 4. Before the statistical analyses of local electoral behavior are undertaken, however, a summary of the socioeconomic and political characteristics of Rhineland-Palatinate is needed, to complete the description of the contextual background of local elections.

RHINELAND-PALATINATE

The state of Rhineland-Palatinate is a postwar creation whose boundaries contain the southern section of the historic Prussian Rhine province and a group of territorial fragments, including parts of Hesse and Hesse-Nassau and the Bavarian Palatine. It is, accordingly, the most heterogeneous of the ten German states. During the Allied occupation, the state was in the French zone.

In terms of land area, Rhineland-Palatinate, with 19,378 kilometers of territory, is one of the small German states, along with Schleswig-Holstein, the Saar, and the city states.[1] In terms of population, it belongs with the small German states also, occupying sixth place in rank: resident population in 1969 was 3,569,000 people.[2] In general, the state is sparsely populated, with 184 inhabitants per kilometer in 1969 (national average: 245), although the aggregate statistics do not adequately portray the diversity within its boundaries.[3]

In 1969, the administrative districts composing the northern-central section of the state, Koblenz and Treves, had population densities of 166 and 100 inhabitants per kilometer. Yet to the south, the Rhine Hesse-Palatinate district, with 266 inhabitants per kilometer, had a denser population structure than the national average.[4] The two largest cities, Mainz and Ludwigshafen, lie in this area, as well as five cities with populations over 40,000.[5] In contrast, Koblenz and Treves are the sole large cities in their respective districts. On the aggregate level, a larger proportion of the population lives in small towns in Rhineland-Palatinate than in Germany as a whole. The state average of 56 per cent Catholic places it as one of the most Catholic German states (national average of Catholic population: 44.5 per cent).[6] The absorption of refugees, a problem for some states, has not been a factor in the political and economic integration of Rhineland-Palatinate. Percentage of refugees in the state population is 7.5 (national average: 15.3).[7]

1. Germany, Federal Statistical Office, *Handbook of Statistics for the Federal Republic of Germany* (hereafter referred to as *Handbook of Statistics*), p. 16.
2. Ibid.
3. Ibid.
4. Ibid.
5. *Statistisches Jahrbuch, 1970*, p. 28.
6. Ibid., p. 39.
7. *Handbook of Statistics*, p. 21.

The state has a relatively weak industrial base, which is reflected in its lower GNP in Deutsche Marken per inhabitant: 7,445 (national average: 8,790).[8] Only two states, Schleswig-Holstein and the Saar, have a lower per inhabitant GNP. The agrarian nature of the economy is clearly apparent. The number of workers engaged in agricultural occupations (17.7 per cent) is higher than the national average (10.3 per cent).[9] Correspondingly, production industries are not as important a sector of the economy in Rhineland-Palatinate as in some other German states, nor do salaried employees and civil servants comprise as high a proportion of the labor force. The importance of agricultural occupations is not surprising, given the geographical position of the state. Both the Rhine and the Mosel wine districts lie partly within the state, and the wine industry plays a very important economic role.

The small-town, agrarian, Catholic composition of the state is closely related to its political history of dominance by parties of the right. The Christian Democrats have been in state power for more than two decades. Their tenure in office, albeit at times with their junior coalition partner, the Free Democrats, has been uninterrupted throughout the postwar period. The Social Democrats have never come close to challenging the CDU leadership. In the 1947–67 state elections, the CDU led the SPD by an average 10 per cent of the votes (45.4 per cent to 35.4 per cent). The gap was narrowed only slightly in the 1971 election, when the SPD received 40.5 per cent of the vote compared to the CDU's 50 per cent.[10]

In terms of national electoral behavior, the picture of CDU strength and SPD weakness is even sharper. The mean vote for the CDU in the 1949–69 national elections was 50.2 per cent, compared to 32.8 per cent for the SPD. How safe a constituency the state is for the CDU may be judged from the observation that the state mean has surpassed the national mean by six percentage points in the period 1949–69. In contrast, the SPD obtained 40 per cent of the vote for the first time in the 1969 election.

8. *Statistisches Jahrbuch, 1970*, p. 495.

9. *Statistisches Jahrbuch, 1968*, p. 128.

10. Information from official publications of Rhineland-Palatinate, *Statistisches Landesamt*, Bad Ems. The results of the eighteen postwar elections discussed in this chapter are contained in the series *Statistik von Rheinland-Pfalz*. The reader is referred to the Bibliography for a full description of individual volumes.

Except for the FDP, which has satisfied the 5 per cent requirement in every national and state election, minor parties have been negligible factors in Rhineland-Palatinate politics. The largest of the other minor parties in the early period, the Communist Party (KPD), received 8.7 per cent of the votes in the first election of 1947 and 6.2 per cent in the 1949 federal election. Its power declined in successive elections before it was banned in 1956.

Most recently, the National Democratic Party (NPD) has been the only other party to surmount the 5 per cent barrier for representation in state elections. With 6.9 per cent of the 1967 state electoral vote, the NPD received *Landtag* seats. Although its vote diminished in the 1969 elections, the party received 5 per cent of the vote in Rhineland-Palatinate, as well as in Hesse, Bavaria, and the Saar. In the 1971 state election, the NPD, with 2.7 per cent of the vote, did not obtain representation.

The party system in Rhineland-Palatinate differs from the national party system in one important respect—exclusion of the SPD as a serious opponent—although one-party rule is characteristic of other German states as well. The preeminence of the CDU may, in turn, be related to the demographic composition of the state. Rhineland-Palatinate is one of the less economically developed German states, with an unusually high Catholic population. The extent to which political parties and voting behavior on the local level diverge from national and state tendencies can be shown only through an examination of municipal election returns. Rhineland-Palatinate, like any other state which might have been chosen for in-depth data analysis, demonstrates some characteristics not necessarily typical of the entire nation. There are, however, several factors which offset the limitations of a single-state study. Most of the analysis presented is bi- or multivariate, not simply descriptive at the aggregate level. The single-state sample offers ample variation in *Gemeinde* units to establish relationships between variables. More important, on the level of individual *Gemeinden*, it is doubtful that interstate differences are significant in terms of this study. For instance, the style of local politics discussed in chapter 2 is similar in all German states. Such cultural contexts do much to nullify whatever socioeconomic differences do exist. Similarly, the continual increase in mobility and communication occurring in all advanced societies has muted both interstate and intrastate differences among *Gemeinden*.

THE LOCAL ENVIRONMENT

The survey data discussed in chapter 2 indicated two important features of *Gemeinde* life: the personally oriented style of politics and the prevalence of nonpartisan political orientations. This local environment is of the utmost relevance to a study of the development of the party system. That the local community has observable effects upon the electoral process has been well documented by students of American politics. Illustrative of these findings is the "breakage effect" hypothesis: other factors being equal, people tend to vote according to the climate of opinion in their home community.[11] Distinctive communal political traditions may thus persist for a long time.

The way the community influences political behavior may be explained in several ways. Angus Campbell argues that community influence derives from the motivation of community members to conform to perceived community norms. In other words, the community itself is a reference group.[12] Robert Putnam advances an alternative explanation. His "social interaction" theory proposes that "community influence is mediated primarily through the numerous personal contacts among members of a community."[13] Thus, even if voters are unaware of communal norms, they may still be influenced by their communal environment. A resident's psychological attachment to his community, or his social involvement in it, may act as transmitter of the community climate of opinion.

These findings have broad implications. Local political activists come under strong influence to adopt the attitudes of the majority community opinion (e.g., nonpartisanship in the case of local German voters).[14] The resistance of a closely knit community(e.g., the small *Gemeinde*) to change will be greater than the resistance of an atomistic community.[15] Residence in the local community may serve as a functional substitute for other means (e.g., the political party) of integrating individuals into the political system.[16] The applicability of

11. Bernard Berelson et al., *Voting*, pp. 98–101.
12. Angus Campbell, "The Political Implications of Community Identification," pp. 318–28.
13. Robert D. Putnam, "Political Attitudes and the Local Community," p. 641.
14. Ibid., p. 653.
15. Ibid.
16. For a discussion of this proposition, see David R. Segal and Marshall W. Meyer, "The Social Context of Political Participation."

these implications to German local electoral behavior is suggested by the statistical data gathered for the Rhineland-Palatinate elections.

TYPES OF ELECTORAL CONTESTS

The very forms of electoral struggle reflect significant local resistance to partisan conflict. Since plurality elections, by definition, are noncompetitive, a prerequisite to partisan politics is the existence of proportional representational electoral systems.[17] Yet approximately one-half of the *Gemeinden* hold plurality elections. Examinations of voting statistics from the six communal elections in Rhineland-Palatinate during the postwar period demonstrate the remarkable entrenchment of plurality contests (Table 6).

TABLE 6
TYPE OF LOCAL ELECTION BY *Gemeinde*

Year	Plurality Elections		PR Elections		Total Elections	
	No.	%	No.	%	No.	%
1948	1,751	60.0	1,162	40.0	2,913	100.0
1952	1,272	43.6	1,642	56.4	2,914	100.0
1956	1,389	47.6	1,527	52.4	2,916	100.0
1960	1,531	53.5	1,385	47.4	2,916	100.0
1964	1,487	51.0	1,431	49.0	2,918	100.0
1969	1,366	52.7	1,225	47.3	2,591	100.0

Noncontested elections bear out the importance of a personalistic style of politics where certain individuals are believed to be the natural communal leaders. Electoral contests in such *Gemeinden* affirm the distinctiveness of the community by institutionalizing informal roles and mores in a political setting.

This peculiarity of local electoral politics has roots in the subjective environment of local voters. The slowness with which local political habits change is encouraged by the cultural norm of preference for harmony as opposed to fractionalization. The ability of a commune to suppress electoral divisions is related to a pervasive social attitude: resistance to change if occasioned by conflict. Desire for harmony in

---

17. If the council seats were contested, there would be two lists submitted, and a PR election would result.

preference to social conflict is widespread in German society.[18] The local setting possesses physical and sociocultural attributes that foster a creation of local harmony.

Complementing this idea of consensus is the feeling that politics is the business of "experts." The preeminence of local notables is reinforced by a cultural stress on the virtue of authority. A long tradition of civic and social leadership by these notables checks the intrusion of more specialized political leadership. Plurality elections thus avoid conflict at the same time as they reinforce communal autonomy. The local consensus precludes the necessity of local electoral competition and conflict.

In this regard, German local politics closely parallel French local politics. Kesselman's research on France suggests some of the ways in which local consensus is maintained and fostered. Efforts to ensure that electoral cleavages do not erode the local consensus often result in a single electoral list. Careful planning through informal processes is reflected in the electoral list's being a microcosm of the alignment of local political forces.[19] Thus, local electoral opposition is avoided, and the sharp cleavages which divide local electorates in national elections do not emerge in local elections. The most important French local officeholder, the mayor, is the chief initiator in fostering communal harmony. The mayor, a local notable par excellence, combines high social status and political power. He acts as the "communal father" and maintains solidarity on local issues through his great prestige.[20]

The overwhelming majority of the *Gemeinden* with no developed organizations for electoral competition are small villages with under three thousand inhabitants; however, two-fifths of the Rhineland-Palatinate people lived in these small communities in 1970.[21] Whether we refer to the number of local governmental units or to the attitudes of the population residing in such units, local politics is very often characterized by the avoidance of electoral conflict. The endurance of local political habits in the midst of the rapid and significant change in postwar Germany testifies to the force of the local community as an influence on voting behavior.

18. Ralf Dahrendorf, "The New Germanies: Restoration, Revolution, Reconstruction," p. 236.
19. Kesselman, pp. 119–35.
20. Ibid., pp. 38ff. For Germany, cf. Pfizer, p. 46, and Ziebill, p. 58.
21. *Statistisches Jahrbuch, 1972*, p. 34.

Withdrawal from political competition is not a characteristic of the half of the *Gemeinden* which have PR elections. Here, in local elections where political parties are present, we might expect local electoral patterns to reflect national. Since organized political groups are a prerequisite for PR elections, political parties as special institutions organized for electoral struggle might well assume a dominant position. An analysis of municipal elections reveals, however, that local influences are still pervasive in the PR elections. Far from being ab-

TABLE 7
PERCENTAGE OF TOTAL VOTE OBTAINED
BY LOCAL VOTER GROUPS

1948	16.7
1952	33.6
1956	31.9
1960	25.9
1964	25.8
1969	25.9

TABLE 8
CHARACTER OF LOCAL ELECTION LISTS

	1948[a]	1952	1956	1960	1964	1969
Local voter group lists	1,295	3,983	4,078	3,302	3,564	3,092
Political party lists	1,738	1,520	1,232	1,361	1,439	1,287
Total lists	3,033	5,503	5,310	4,663	5,003	4,379

a. Total number of lists was not available; statistics are for lists in PR elections only.

sorbed by the political parties, local voter groups show amazing perseverance as electoral competitors. Their share of local votes has, in fact, increased over the years, as Table 7 demonstrates. With the exception of the first election in 1948, local voter groups have obtained at least one-fourth of the vote in every election. The consistency of this vote seems to imply that local voter groups are quite firmly entrenched.

The extreme activeness of local voter groups is apparent when we compare the number of nomination lists submitted by local voter groups and by political parties (Table 8). Local voter groups submit approximately three times as many lists as all political parties combined.

Since about one-half of the elections in any one year are plurality contests, a high degree of competition is indicated in the PR elections. The distribution of lists in the 1952 elections, in which local voter group lists formed 72 per cent of the lists submitted, is indicative of the number of local groups entering the elections (Table 9). Electoral

TABLE 9
DISTRIBUTION OF LOCAL ELECTION LISTS
IN PR ELECTIONS BY *Gemeinde*

	Number	Percentage
With 2 lists	700	42.6
With 3 lists	477	29.0
With 4 lists	276	16.8
With 5 lists	123	7.5
With 6+ lists	66	4.1
Total no. of *Gemeinden*	1,642	100.0

competition is not confined to partisan politics. The increase in local voter group lists and the decrease in political party lists, as shown in Table 8, is symptomatic of continuing local resistance to partisan conflict.

THE ELECTORAL POSITION OF POLITICAL PARTIES

Political parties have been unable to make any significant inroads into local elections over a twenty-one-year period. As Table 10 shows, political parties actually contested more elections in 1948 than in 1969. The local activeness of political parties in the first election conforms to general tendencies. The role of political parties in satisfying material needs and self-interest was greatest in the immediate postwar years. In the 1950s as normalization of personal lives occurred, a trend away from political involvement toward privacy developed.[22]

Political parties compete in less than one-fourth of the local contests.[23] Lists of minor parties are negligible in local elections. The FDP

22. Hartenstein and Liepelt, pp. 46–47. See also Sidney Verba, "Germany: The Remaking of a Political Culture," p. 164. For the decline of parties on the local level in Hesse, see Ruediger, pp. 90–91.
23. Statistics were not available for the 1948 elections.

is the only party consistently to contest more elections in successive years, but it still plays a minimal role in local politics. The number of electoral lists of the CDU has declined while the number of SPD lists has increased. These trends may be related to the local organizational strategies of the parties.

The founding initiative for local CDU organizations was from religious persons whose main interest was "Rettung der Gemeinde."[24] Their efforts, in other words, derived from *Gemeinde* interests and not from a preconceived party position. Officials from upper level CDU party organizations did not come into the communes until later. In fact, as the CDU developed into a more defined party politically, local difficulties arose. Many communal leaders who were interested in *Gemeinde* concerns but wished to remain political neutrals withdrew.

TABLE 10
PERCENTAGE OF LOCAL ELECTIONS CONTESTED
BY POLITICAL PARTIES

Party	1952	1956	1960	1964	1969
CDU	24.1	20.9	22.2	22.7	20.8
SPD	18.9	17.6	19.8	21.6	23.4
FDP	3.0	3.1	4.3	4.8	5.1
KPD	5.2				

In contrast, local SPD organizations were from the beginning in close contact with higher level officials. There were reciprocal meetings between communal, county, and higher level party officials. A relatively tight organization was characteristic of the SPD down to the local level.[25]

The distribution of political party lists is closely related to the distribution of the electoral strength of the political parties (Table 11). Political parties were strongest in the 1948 election. After a loss of 11 per cent of the total vote in 1952, parties have steadily and very slowly recovered, but nonetheless they have yet to equal their first electoral showing. The partisan gains derive mainly from the increase in the SPD vote, since the CDU and FDP have not regained their 1948 levels.[26] The local positions of the CDU and SPD are thus reversed

24. Pflaum, p. 254.
25. Ibid., pp. 253–54.
26. The FDP shows considerable local strength in some other states. For

from their state and national electoral positions in Rhineland-Palatinate.
Within the boundaries of partisan politics is a dominant two-party system. The CDU and SPD contest the greatest number of elections and obtain the great majority of partisan votes. This development is far less dramatic in local than in national and state elections. The combined strength of the CDU and SPD increased by only 4 per cent between 1948 and 1969, from 51.4 per cent to 55.4 per cent. In contrast with what has happened at national and state levels, the CDU and SPD have not benefited from the decline of minority parties. Such parties have never been a factor in local elections.

TABLE 11
PERCENTAGE OF TOTAL VOTE OBTAINED BY
POLITICAL PARTIES IN LOCAL ELECTIONS

Year	CDU	SPD	FDP	Other	All Parties Combined
1948	26.2	25.2	5.3	5.6	62.3
1952	20.7	22.6	5.1	2.9	51.3
1956	22.1	26.4	4.1	0.5	53.1
1960	25.5	26.1	5.1	0.4	57.1
1964	25.6	29.5	4.1	0.1	59.3
1969	26.0	29.4	4.0	1.1	60.5

Figure 1 shows the comparative combined strength of the CDU and SPD at the various levels of electoral politics. The gap between local and national or state strength has increased over the years, so that in 1969 the CDU and SPD obtained one-third more of the vote in the national election than in the local elections. Local electorates do not divide in the same way as do national and state electorates. Competition for voters occurs not so much between the parties as between political parties and local voter groups.

In German local elections, the important issue is not so much the development of a two-party system as the establishment of the party system itself. Since political parties obtain only slightly over one-half of the local vote, a huge reservoir of unmobilized partisan voters remains. Local electorates demonstrate amazing continuity in keeping political parties out of local politics.

---

instance, the party polled 32.4 per cent of the vote in the 1952 local elections as compared to only 15.8 per cent of the 1953 *Bundestag* vote in the same villages in North Rhine–Westphalia. Pflaum, p. 271.

FIGURE 1

COMBINED STRENGTH OF CDU AND SPD, 1947–69, IN PERCENTAGE OF TOTAL VOTE

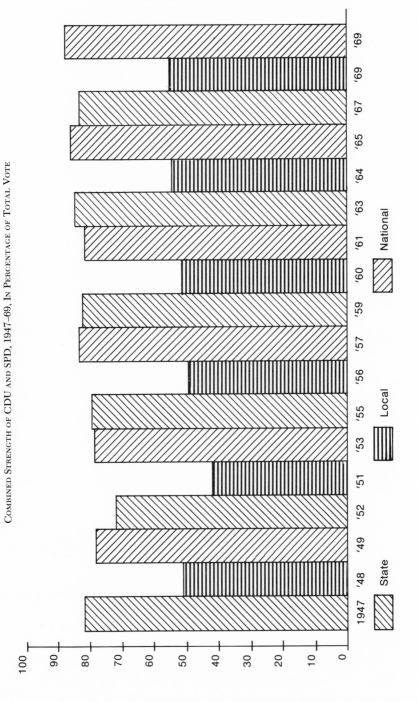

During a twenty-one-year period, these electorates consistently maintained their nonpartisanship by means of plurality elections and the submission of local voter group lists in PR elections. The dramatic fluctuations in party strength according to level of government are demonstrated in Figure 2.

THE GOVERNMENTAL POSITION OF POLITICAL PARTIES

The circumscription of the role of political parties at the grass-roots level of the German political system is even greater in the case of officeholders than in the case of competitors for office. Structurally, the *Gemeinde* has a high proportion of formal political roles. In 1964, the ratio of local council members to the total electorate was 1:82. In contrast, the ratios for *Landtag* and *Bundestag* deputies were 1:2,363 and 1:76,226 respectively. The sheer number of local openings for direct political participation suggests that there is great opportunity for the clear demonstration of the desires of the populace and the trends those desires may exhibit. Most important, perhaps, they increase the opportunity for direct contact between leaders and followers.

In the operations of local government, personal relationships assume a vital role, the importance of which is magnified in small *Gemeinden* through the allocation of council seats. The proportion of seats allocated to *Gemeinden* of increasing size is smaller than the proportional increase in the number of inhabitants. At one end of the continuum, a tiny village may elect one council member for every twenty voters. At the opposite end of the continuum, a large city may elect one council member for every 350 voters.[27]

This scheme of allocation results in vote-seat discrepancies, to the detriment of political parties. The local consequences are the opposite of the national. In national elections, the major parties usually reap a larger proportion of *Bundestag* seats than votes because of the 5 per cent clause. Parties obtaining less than 5 per cent of the vote do not share in the allocation of seats. The surplus seats fall mainly to the CDU/CSU and the SPD. The CDU/CSU's and SPD's percentages of seats over their percentages of votes averaged 3.4 per cent and 2.3 per cent, respectively, in the 1949–69 elections. In local elections,

27. The allocation of council seats by size of *Gemeinde* is given in Appendix C.

FIGURE 2

PERCENTAGE OF TOTAL VOTE OBTAINED BY MAJOR PARTIES, 1947–69

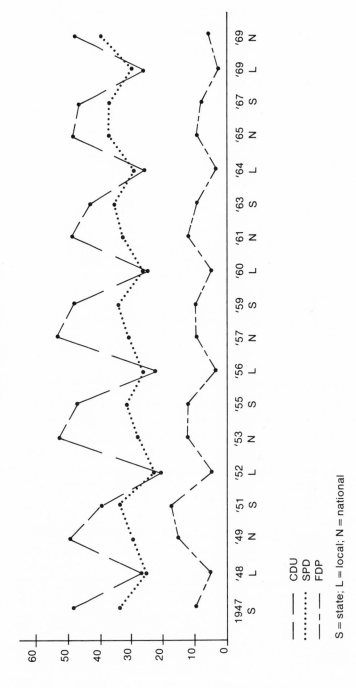

CDU
SPD
FDP

S = state; L = local; N = national

the major parties do not achieve the number of council seats that their share of the total vote would indicate because of the numerous small towns with no partisan candidates. For instance, in 1964, partisans occupied barely one-fourth of the total number of local council seats. Independent candidates held two-fifths of the seats, and representatives of local voter groups held another one-third. Table 12 presents the distribution of local council seats by affiliation of councilors.

TABLE 12
DISTRIBUTION OF LOCAL COUNCIL SEATS CONTRASTED
TO DISTRIBUTION OF TOTAL VOTE, 1964
(in percentages)

	Seats	Votes
CDU	12.8	25.6
SPD	12.1	29.5
FDP	1.0	4.1
Other parties		0.1
Voter groups	35.3	25.8
Independents	38.8	14.8
Total[a]	100.0	100.0

a. Total number of seats = 28,854; total number of voters = 2,363,000.

The number of seats occupied is a relevant factor in the discussion of party strength in that the aim of political parties in electoral contests is to win power. As illustrated in Table 12, the nonpartisan character of local politics is more noticeable in the structure of government, i.e., percentage of local councilors, than in the structure of electoral competition, i.e., percentage of total vote.

LOCAL ELECTORATES IN PERSPECTIVE

A discussion of voter participation has thus far been omitted. An avoidance of politics in the sense of partisan involvement could possibly be one dimension of withdrawal from political activity in a more general sense. Yet citizen involvement in politics as measured by the act of voting is comparatively high. Although somewhat lower than in national elections, voter turnout in local elections is, in fact, generally higher than in state elections, as Figure 3 demonstrates. Social pressure or interest in local concerns is sufficient to mobilize voters

FIGURE 3

VOTER TURNOUT, 1947–69

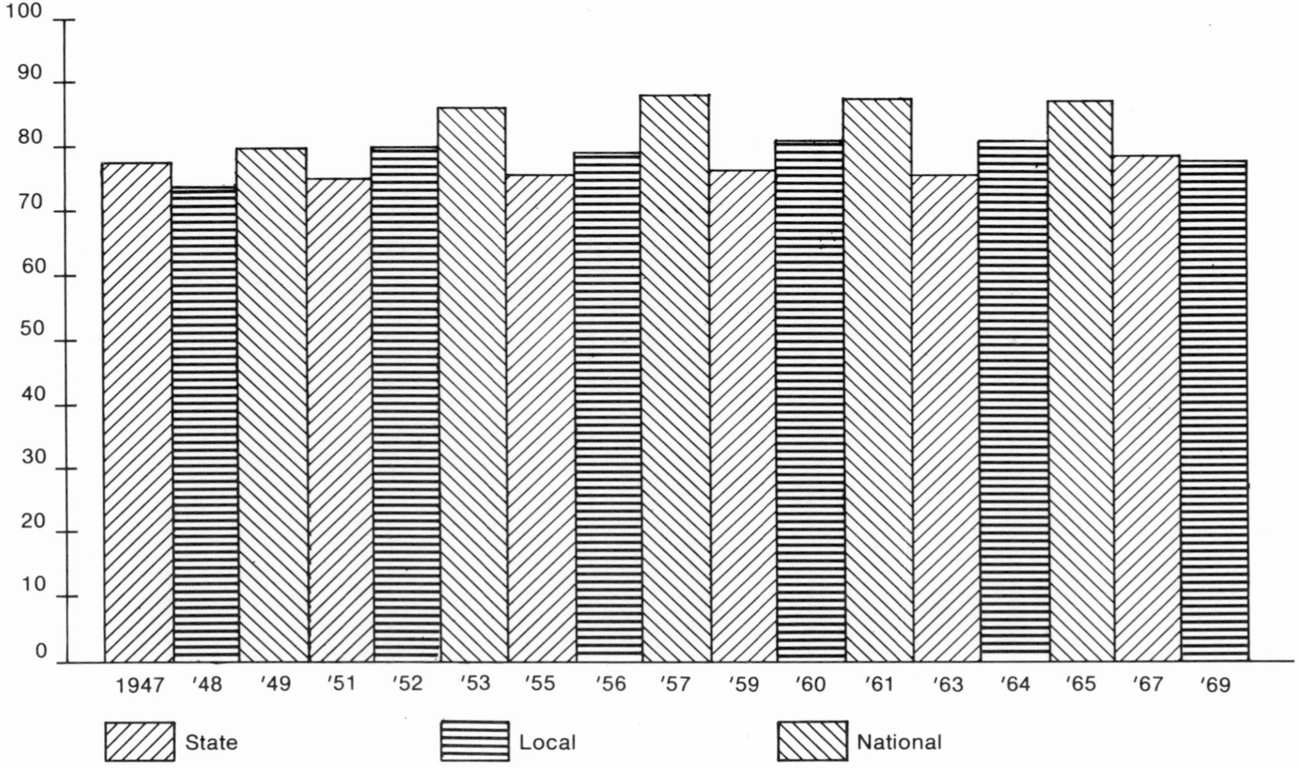

in the absence of either partisan conflict or the anticipated closeness of an election.

An examination of local electoral behavior confirms the accuracy of responses to the surveys discussed in the preceding chapter. People believe that communal tasks may be performed without the intervention of political parties. High interest in local government is reflected in voter turnout and in the numerous local voter group lists.

The specific style of electoral politics is related to the size of the municipality. The smallest villages maintain communal autonomy and consensus by rejecting any form of electoral conflict. Elections confirm the informal selection of communal leaders. The larger towns, in contrast, have quite competitive electoral contests to choose their government officials. This competition is often conducted through local voter groups. In short, the interest in and the competitiveness of local electoral politics occur to a great extent without explicit partisan politics.

The nonpartisanship of German local elections should not be confused with the American phenomenon of nonpartisan municipal elections. The contexts set by the electoral systems are quite different. The American system is based on the premise that political parties should not participate and legally bars the use of party labels on the ballot. In contrast, the role of political parties in Germany is legally recognized and encouraged through the local electoral laws. If a party label does not appear on a German local ballot, the determining factor lies elsewhere than in the electoral code. The presence of political parties, in other words, is expected in German municipal elections rather than discouraged. Yet the long histories and traditions of self-government, the prominence of personal relationships, the discrediting of political parties as disrupters of local harmony and as intruders upon local autonomy combine to produce the significant impact of local political habits upon the electoral process. The *Gemeinde* possesses many characteristics to set it apart as an independent constituency. In such a context there is no easy projection of national political party organizations into local politics and no automatic transfer of national and state electoral loyalties.

The preceding analysis constitutes the preliminary step in this study of local electoral politics. To determine the sources of support for party systems, we must identify the local conditions most conducive to partisan conflict. Through an examination of the social, political, and economic differences in *Gemeinden*, the relationship of varying structured contexts of electoral behavior to the party system may be determined. Our perspective changes: from analysis of the *Gemeinden* as entities distinct from other elements in the national system, we turn to analysis of the variation among *Gemeinden* in rates and directions of electoral change.

4. The Politicization of Local Elections

THE different forms of electoral politics in the national and local arenas call for different research strategies. Since the party system constitutes a "given" in national voting behavior, research concentrates primarily on the analysis of changes in voter support among the established parties. At the local level of electoral politics, a developed party system has yet to emerge. Accordingly, our research focuses first on the contexts in which electoral cleavages develop and are maintained; e.g., we ask what *Gemeinde* characteristics are associated with plurality and PR elections, local voter group entrenchment, and the entry of political parties. Once political parties have entered local elections, do they become entrenched or do they disappear? What is the sequence and what is the timing?

A large body of comparative research suggests that partisan politics is the dependent variable. Parties may be viewed as the outgrowth of the processes of social and economic change, and for the establishment of parties, fundamental conditions must first be met.[1] Thus, we must ask what types of change are most conducive to the local formation of political parties. In the attempt to ascertain the range of conditions supportive of a local party system in Germany we shall, therefore, consider the political, socioeconomic, and cultural structures of *Gemeinden* as possible independent variables.

The official election statistics discussed previously are based upon published totals of elections in all *Gemeinden*. Reliance on these totals for information about local electorates may produce the very fallacy of aggregation that prompted this research. Differences among *Gemeinden* are masked since all are included together. Furthermore, much vital information is excluded from the official totals. A community-to-community analysis through time is necessary if we are to

1. LaPalombara and Weiner, especially the introductory chapter.

avoid the dilemmas of unjustified generalizations and answer many unresolved questions about the nature of the local electorate.

A 20 per cent systematic sample is the basis for the following examination of local electorates in varying socioeconomic and political settings in Rhineland-Palatinate.[2] For each *Gemeinde*, information was gathered on the total electorate, on voter turnout, on votes cast for individual parties, on the number of council seats being contested in local elections, and on numerous socioeconomic indicators.

Given the difficulties of preparing raw data for processing and analysis, discussed in chapter 3, the comparative community study of local electorates in Rhineland-Palatinate is possible for four local elections and all state and national elections through 1967. In the data analysis, the first local elections of 1948 are excluded because municipal electoral returns were officially published only for *Gemeinden* of more than two thousand inhabitants—less than one-fifth of the municipalities. Boundary changes resulting from mergers or dissolution of *Gemeinden* further complicate time-series analysis. Through the local government reorganizational act of 1968, more than three hundred municipalities were dissolved and merged into others. The magnitude of these boundary changes necessitated the exclusion of the 1969 elections.

Levels of Politicization

For the study of the dynamics of party development, information about communes at varying levels of electoral competition was gathered. One means of evaluating the spread of partisan politics in local communities is examination of the number and character of electoral lists by *Gemeinde*. The reaching out of the party system into new territory characterizes the process of politicization, "the breakdown of the traditional system of local rule through the entry of nationally organized parties into municipal elections."[3]

The crucial first step is the transition from plurality to PR elections. Instead of unaffiliated candidates, competitive lists of groups organized for electoral struggle characterize the ballot. A PR electoral sys-

---

2. We observed no periodic tendency in the list from which the sample was selected. To check further for any systematic bias, we compared sample characteristics with universe characteristics.
3. Rokkan, "Electoral Mobilization," p. 244.

tem provides an entry for partisan politics into local government. Local notables must now organize into groups in order to obtain political office. This first change by no means ensures that electoral competitors include political parties; many contests remain exclusively in the domain of local voter groups. The initial thrust toward partisan politics occurs when one nationally organized political party enters local elections. The next step is the introduction of additional party lists— although local voter group lists still remain. Full politicization occurs only when all lists are of national political parties.

To distinguish among communes with different forms of electoral lists and competition, we categorized local elections into five levels of politicization: those with one or no list, plurality elections; those with two or more local voter group lists; those with one party list and one or more local voter group lists; those with two or more party lists and one or more local voter group lists; and those with party lists only.[4]

The gradualness of the politicizing process is already apparent from our knowledge that a majority of *Gemeinden* maintain plurality elections and that local voter group lists predominate in PR elections. Table 13 demonstrates the actual progression of politicization in four local elections.

The process of politicization is neither a unilateral process nor a process which contains a momentum of its own. Although the number of *Gemeinden* reaching full politicization increased slightly, the number of *Gemeinden* reverting to the prepoliticized stage increased dramatically. Local voter groups monopolize one-fifth of the elections. Communes at either a very low level or an intermediate stage of politicization comprise one-fourth. A mere 3 per cent of the communes engage in purely partisan electoral politics.[5]

The slowness with which local political habits change and the ability of local voters to synthesize communal norms with modern structures delay the process of politicization. Exclusion of political parties from local government is the norm. Even after the entry of national party organizations into local settings, resistance to partisan politics

4. These five levels of politicization are used by Rokkan in his analyses of Norwegian local electorates. See "Electoral Mobilization," pp. 250–53, and Rokkan and Valen, "The Mobilization of the Periphery," pp. 191–99.
5. Norwegian communal politics contrast sharply with German in levels of politicization. In 1963, a mere 2.1 per cent of Norwegian communes held plurality elections, compared to 55.7 per cent with party lists only. Rokkan, "Electoral Mobilization," p. 251.

continues unabated. The stability of the number of *Gemeinden* maintaining local voter groups in the presence of two or more political parties indicates that voter groups remain significant electoral competitors.

FLUCTUATIONS IN LEVELS OF POLITICIZATION

Although movement toward partisan politics is not automatic, changes in politicization do occur, and we may measure them by comparing electoral list alternatives in consecutive elections, by *Gemeinde*. Of particular interest are questions concerning the magnitude and direc-

TABLE 13
PROCESS OF POLITICIZATION IN LOCAL ELECTIONS, 1952–64
(in percentages)

Electoral Option	1952	1956	1960	1964
1 or no list, plurality election	44.1	49.0	55.0	52.4
2 or more local voter group lists	28.6	26.7	20.3	20.8
1 party list, 1 or more local voter group lists	14.1	12.0	10.6	12.0
2 or more party lists, 1 or more local voter group lists	10.8	10.4	10.8	11.5
Party lists only	2.4	1.9	3.3	3.3
Total no. of *Gemeinden* = 576				

tion of change. What proportion of *Gemeinden* maintain one level of politicization over time? What proportion manifest changes? What levels of politicization are most susceptible to change?

In the 1956 election, 176 of the 576 communes were at another level of politicization than in the 1952 election. One hundred fifty-eight communes experienced electoral list changes between the 1956 and 1960 elections, and 133 between the 1960 and 1964 elections. Although fewer communes deviated from their past pattern in each successive election, at least one-fifth fluctuated in their type of electoral competition. The nature of the changes in levels of politicization is portrayed in Table 14.

Plurality contests are the least susceptible to change. Less than one-fifth of the communes in the prepoliticized stage advanced to any form of competitive or partisan politics. A *Gemeinde* must switch to a PR

electoral system before any significant change appears. In the PR elections, the most volatile stage of politicization occurs when one party
list is introduced along with local voter group lists. One-half to two-
fifths of communes at this level did not remain there in successive
elections. The greatest fluctuations take place in the fully politicized
contests. Almost three-fourths of the *Gemeinden* holding purely partisan elections in 1952 did not hold such elections in 1956. In 1964,
however, approximately three-fifths of the *Gemeinden* at the level of
complete politicization maintained that level.

TABLE 14
Changes in Level of Politicization
in Local Elections by *Gemeinden*
(in percentages)

Gemeinden Changing from:	1952–56	1956–60	1960–64
1 or no list, plurality election	16.5	13.8	17.0
2 or more local voter group lists	34.5	44.8	31.6
1 party list, 1 or more local voter group lists	51.9	47.8	39.3
2 or more party lists, 1 or more local voter group lists	33.9	23.3	17.7
Party lists only	71.4	27.3	36.8

A further examination of the communes with PR elections which
changed in the character of their electoral lists suggests that many ob-
stacles still confront the movement toward partisan politics. Of the
one-third to two-fifths of the *Gemeinden* in each election that changed
from having local voter group lists only, more than 75 per cent went
back to noncompetitive plurality elections. The tendency to switch to
a lower level of politicization characterizes the changes in the three
categories of partisan elections as well. Thus in three-fourths of the
communes with one party list on the ballot to begin with, the party
list disappeared in successive elections. The drop-out rate of political
parties is quite high at the low level of politicization. In *Gemeinden*
experiencing change, the odds are 3 to 1 for the disappearance of the
one party and against the introduction of additional parties.

In partisan contests, the intermediate level of politicization, in which
two or more political parties are present along with local voter groups,
is the most stable. Something of a standoff occurs between voter groups
and parties. Local voter groups remain in the path of partisan politics occasioned by the presence of at least two political parties. When

change does occur, for the first time it is almost as apt to be in the direction of partisan engagement as away from it. Forty-six per cent of the group of communes which changed in 1964 entered into purely partisan elections. Yet if we consider the number of changes in *Gemeinden* with only party list alternatives, the resilience of local voter groups is apparent. In 1964, local voter groups entered lists in 36.8 per cent of the communes whose lists had been monopolized by political parties in 1960. Exclusion of local groups from electoral competition does not prevent their penetration in a later election.

The fragility of partisan electoral list alternatives over time implies that certain structural conditions are a prerequisite to the sustaining of partisan divisions. We wish, therefore, to examine the relationship between forms of electoral competition and other communal characteristics. The size of the *Gemeinde* is the first factor that we will evaluate. All *Gemeinden* were stratified into six categories of population. Concurrent data were available for each local election.

The Kendall rank-order correlation coefficients of politicization with *Gemeinde* size are .54 in the 1952, 1956, and 1960 elections and .57 in the 1964 election (significance level .001). This strong association between size of community and politicization is demonstrated in Table 15.

The tiny hamlets of fewer than 150 inhabitants are marked by the almost pure elimination of competition. Villages with populations to 500 overwhelmingly maintain nonpartisan politics, but the beginning of fractionalization into groups of local citizens occurs. Noncompetitive elections fall under 50 per cent for the first time in communes of 500 to 1,000 inhabitants, and one-fourth have some form of partisan elections, primarily of only one party lists. The most diverse group and the one where political parties make their first breakthrough is that of the *Gemeinden* of 1,000 to 3,000. In towns with 3,000 and more inhabitants, partisan politics are entrenched, albeit in a limited form since local voter groups compete against parties in most of these towns.

STRUCTURAL CONDITIONS FOR POLITICIZATION: CULTURAL

The size of a *Gemeinde* indicates a cultural phenomenon which does much to explain the slowness of the politicization process. The smaller the commune, the more important face-to-face contacts and informal roles. For the country dweller, a small commune may act as a "quasigroup" reference structure much like his urban counterpart's occupational role.[6] When personal relationships are the basis of communal life, political conflict is easily translated into personal strife. It becomes important to protect communal harmony against outside divisive forces such as political parties.[7] The act of voting formally sanctions the role of local notables—persons who have shown their leadership

TABLE 15
LEVEL OF POLITICIZATION BY SIZE OF *Gemeinde*
(in percentages)

Electoral Options	Number of Inhabitants					
	Under 150	150–500	500–1,000	1,000–3,000	3,000–10,000	Over 10,000
1952 election						
1 or no list	86.4	55.0	33.3	7.7	3.7	
2 or more local lists	9.1	37.3	34.8	16.7		
1 party + local lists	4.5	6.5	27.0	29.5		
2 party + local lists		0.4	3.5	39.7	81.5	75.0
Party lists only		0.8	1.4	6.4	14.8	25.0
	100.0	100.0	100.0	100.0	100.0	100.0
Total *Gemeinden*	66	260	141	78	27	4
1964 election						
1 or no list	91.0	68.3	43.8	10.0	3.3	
2 or more local lists	9.0	26.4	26.7	12.5		
1 party + local lists		4.9	21.9	30.0	3.3	
2 party + local lists		0.4	5.5	43.8	56.7	71.4
Party lists only			2.1	3.8	36.7	28.6
	100.0	100.0	100.0	100.0	100.0	100.0
Total *Gemeinden*	67	246	146	80	30	7

qualities through other areas of communal life. The political relationship is only one of the social relationships of the village. Divisions that do occur are kept primarily local. Notables organize their own local groups to submit election lists, and the cleavages introduced by partisan politics are avoided.

Our inference that small *Gemeinden* function as quasi-groups in voting behavior cannot be directly validated by ecological data; how-

6. Erwin K. Scheuch, "Social Context and Individual Behavior," p. 150.
7. For a discussion of how communal harmony is achieved in France, see Kesselman's study.

ever, survey data from other sources lend support to this belief. One German study concluded "in small communities [fewer than 1,000 inhabitants] participation in politics is not behavior functionally differentiated from other behavior."[8] Switches in voting behavior occurred, regardless of change in demographic characteristics of these *Gemeinden*, only when local notables changed their commitment. In other words, in the midst of social or class division in small communes political consensus remains as long as the traditional leaders command the loyalty of local followers.[9]

STRUCTURAL CONDITIONS FOR POLITICIZATION: SOCIOECONOMIC

As a *Gemeinde* becomes larger, the possibility of cleavages and issues for partisan division increases. In *Gemeinden* with more differentiated economies and less homogeneous social groups, new, functionally specific leadership groups compete with traditional ones, occasioning a split in previously monolithic leadership groups or the alliance of local notables with outside groups. The effects of economic development upon partisan development are suggested in Table 16.

The *Gemeinden* with partisan elections possess more of the indicators of industrialization and urbanization than do the *Gemeinden* with nonpartisan elections. This evidence is in the mainstream of the information gathered on the effects of industrialization and urbanization on partisan politics in Norway and other countries. In the words of Stein Rokkan: "The lower the density, the smaller the communities, the less developed and differentiated the economy, the more personal and territorial the style of representation and the less developed the organizations for local electoral competition."[10]

Since local voter groups are present in the overwhelming majority of partisan elections, the data in Table 16 possibly indicate mere frac-

8. Scheuch, p. 153. For France, see Tarrow, "The Urban-Rural Cleavage," p. 356.
9. This phenomenon of personalized relations has been defined as political clientelism. A number of studies show that such a traditional system of personal relationships persists in many countries behind the facade of modern political institutions, e.g., voting. See Sidney Tarrow, *Peasant Communism in Southern Italy*, and Rene Lemarchand and Keith Legg, "Political Clientelism and Development."
10. Rokkan, "Methods and Models in the Comparative Study of Nation-Building," p. 89.

tionalization of electorates. Political parties may not be the primary electoral organizations. An increase in the diversity and complexity of communal life may not necessarily ensure that people seek representation of their sectional interests in political parties.[11] For the investigation of the sociological bases that sustain party conflict, a more refined concept of partisan politics is needed than knowledge of the incidence of party lists in local elections.

TABLE 16
ECONOMIC CHARACTERISTICS OF *Gemeinden* WITH NONPARTISAN
AND PARTISAN ELECTIONS IN 1964[a]

Characteristic	Nonpartisan Elections[b]	Partisan Elections[c]
Population density		
(per sq. km.)	86	241
Employment structure		
% white collar workers and civil servants	7.9	16.7
% manual workers	32.9	42.2
% self-employed	22.0	17.4
% female	42.5	38.1
% commuters (*Auspendler*)[d]	34.8	42.4
(*Einpendler*)[e]	8.4	17.7
Primary income sources		
of the population		
% agriculture[f]	51.4	27.7
% production	30.8	41.8
% trade	8.2	14.3
% services	9.6	16.1
Local government viability		
Community tax strength		
(DM per inhabitant)	40.8	79.6
Kms. of municipal streets	3.3	9.1
	N = 322	N = 154

a. Calculations of economic variables are based on 1961 census data.
b. Includes plurality elections and PR elections with only local voter groups.
c. Includes all PR elections with one party or more.
d. *Auspendler*: outward-bound daily commuters.
e. *Einpendler*: inward-bound daily commuters.
f. Includes forestry and fishing.

11. Regional analyses of Norwegian communes showed that sharp differences in levels of politicization existed among communes with similar socioeconomic characteristics. See Rokkan, "Electoral Mobilization," pp. 252–53.

An index of partisan mobilization was created to measure the strength of political parties in local elections.[12] Pearson product-moment correlation coefficients were calculated for partisan mobilization with various socioeconomic growth characteristics of the *Gemeinden.* The correlations are given in Table 17.

TABLE 17
CORRELATES OF PARTISAN MOBILIZATION
IN LOCAL ELECTIONS, 1956–64[a]

Economic Variable	1964	1960	1956
White collar workers and civil servants	.58	.57	.56
Population density	.57	.58	.56
Agriculture	−.52	−.53	−.50
Trade	.48	.48	.47
Population size	.45	.44	.45
Municipal streets	.42	.39	.39
Services	.38	.36	.30
Community tax strength	.36	.34	.33
Einpendler	.36	.36	.33
Self-employed	−.36	−.37	−.34
Population change[b]	.35	.36	.32
Production	.33	.36	.36
Manual workers	.31	.32	.31
Female employees	−.31	−.34	−.31
Auspendler	.18	.21	.19

a. Demographic variables are calculated from 1961 census data. The Pearson product-moment correlation coefficients are significant at the .001 level.
b. Change in size of population of *Gemeinde* between 1950 and 1961.

The main demographic correlates of partisan mobilization in local elections are civil servants and white collar workers, population density, and work force in agriculture. *Gemeinden* combine rural and urban components in varying proportions, but the vast majority of *Gemeinden* are located at the rural end of the spectrum. The inhibiting influence of the *Gemeinde* on partisan mobilization stems from structural features which complement the cultural dimension discussed

12. The index of partisan mobilization is calculated thus:

$$\text{Index} = \frac{p_1 + p_2 + \cdots p_n}{\text{total vote}} \cdot 100$$

p = party; the value of the index ranges from 0 to 100. A value of 100 indicates full partisan mobilization; thus, as the percentage of votes cast for local voter groups declines, the value of the index increases.

above. Change is occurring in the socioeconomic sphere, but the nature of this change is what is crucial for partisan mobilization. A common form of economic growth in communes is the abandoning of agriculture for more profitable occupations. Increasingly the small-town dwellers are becoming commuters (*Auspendler*) working in industrial enterprises. The communes then are becoming less isolated culturally and more differentiated economically and socially.

Yet demographic indicators of the type of change actually occurring are more weakly associated with partisan mobilization (manual workers .31, *Auspendler* .18) than are the indicators of urbanization (white collar workers and civil servants .58, population density .57). The urban structural conditions most conducive to partisan mobilization are missing *ipso facto* from most *Gemeinden* because of the nature of local governmental units.

For examination of the relationship of *Gemeinde* socioeconomic characteristics to partisan mobilization, multiple stepwise regression analysis was utilized. The cumulative effect of the demographic variables is seen in Table 18.[13]

TABLE 18
MULTIPLE STEPWISE REGRESSION OF PARTISAN
MOBILIZATION IN LOCAL ELECTIONS, 1964[a]

Independent Variable	Multiple R	Variance Accounted For
White collar workers and civil servants	.579	.336
Population density	.630	.396
Catholics	.637	.405
Agriculture	.642	.413

a. Demographic variables are calculated from 1961 census data. All correlations are significant beyond the .001 level.

Combining the two indicators of urbanization (white collar workers and civil servants, and population density) accounts for approximately 40 per cent of the variance. The proportion of the work force in white collar occupations remains the most important index of partisan mobilization.

13. More variables than are given in the table were statistically significant, but they did not contribute any theoretical significance, and therefore were omitted.

Our investigation of the structural conditions for partisan mobilization suggests that the relationship of socioeconomic development to party development is more complex than is commonly thought. *Although economic growth may encourage social and political fractionalization, a specific constellation of socioeconomic components sustains partisan competition.* To evaluate this hypothesis, factor analysis was employed to obtain summary measures of socioeconomic development so that we could separate the key factors from one another. The rotated factors of the socioeconomic variables reveal three distinct dimensions (Table 19).[14]

TABLE 19
ROTATED FACTORS OF SOCIOECONOMIC VARIABLES

	I	II	III
Manual workers	.919	.176	.073
Production	.893	.145	.159
Auspendler	.861	.106	−.211
Self-employed	−.751	−.294	−.129
Agriculture	−.743	−.630	−.182
Female employees	−.570	−.357	−.036
White collar workers and civil servants	.298	.859	.276
Services	.080	.657	.163
Trade	.299	.654	.126
Einpendler	.202	.605	.230
Community tax strength	.058	.520	.307
Population size	.060	.252	.937
Municipal streets	.003	.179	.830
Population density	.263	.455	.667
% of explained variance	66.5	24.3	9.2

We identify the first factor as the industrial dimension of socioeconomic development. It shows high loadings of indicators of industrial occupations and a corresponding decrease of the agricultural indicators. The second factor can be termed the tertiary dimension of socioeconomic development since its high correlates reflect the presence of services, public administration, and trade, and their expansion in the economy. The third factor is identified as the size dimension. The

14. The factor analyses in this research were calculated using the Statistical Package for the Social Sciences (SPSS) principal factor solution with iteration and varimax orthogonal rotation. The intercorrelation matrix of the variables entered in the factor analysis is given in Appendix D.

reader will note from Table 18 that these three dimensions are represented in the first four variables in the multiple stepwise regression.

To ascertain the relationship of partisan mobilization to each of the socioeconomic dimensions, we performed a separate factor analysis. The loadings for partisan mobilization are .197 on the industrial factor, .469 on the tertiary factor, and .382 on the size factor.[15] The nature of the loadings supports the hypothesis derived from the previous analysis. Partisan mobilization is linked to a tertiary economy and to larger political units—characteristics of urban society and a modern economy. The urbanization process can, therefore, be separated into a size component and two economic components.

When we distinguish levels of socioeconomic growth, we may better account for the stability and endurance of local political habits in the midst of rapid environmental change. The industrial dimension, most typical of the change in communal structural development, is the least associated with partisan mobilization. The key to communal partisan mobilization is in the level of socioeconomic development rather than in the process of general socioeconomic development.

Our analysis of German local electorates suggests a corollary to the general conclusions of comparative research on party system development. The importance of the relationship of socioeconomic development to partisan mobilization has previously been conceived mainly in terms of the process.[16] Since the crucial factor for partisan mobilization in other countries was the change from a primary economy, further investigation among levels of economic growth was superfluous. For example, by 1947 fewer than 10 per cent of Norwegian rural communes were holding nonpartisan local elections.[17] Full politicization of Swedish rural communes occurred even earlier; 80 per cent had purely partisan elections in 1938.[18] Yet in Germany, where partisan mobilization has made small inroads into local electoral behavior, the process of economic change stands in second place to the specific type of economic change.

15. The factor analysis was recomputed in order to include political variables, but there was little change in the factors themselves. The same dimensions were clearly identifiable and even the loadings of the socioeconomic variables showed almost undetectable changes.
16. See Rokkan, "Electoral Mobilization."
17. Ibid., p. 251.
18. Ibid., p. 261.

5. Electoral Participation

W E NOTED earlier that involvement as measured by the act of voting is rather high in local elections. We now wish to examine the relationship of voter participation to communal elections in more depth. Voting is important because it is the sole act of participation in politics for most citizens in most countries.

An investigation of voting turnout by levels of elections and by type of electoral contests may be particularly valuable in sorting out some of the many theories about electoral participation. Research in the United States and other countries has shown that national elections attract the most attention, that partisans are more likely to vote than are nonpartisans, that competition stimulates turnout on election day, and that the motivation to vote is dependent upon perceived closeness of the vote.[1] Yet, recent communal research in at least one European country calls into question most of the above inferences. French local electoral turnout is higher than national electoral turnout. This high interest in municipal elections is coupled with low competition for office and low partisan involvement.[2]

We cannot evaluate individual intentions and motivations through ecological data, but we can discuss electorates in terms of recurring patterns in voter turnout. Our sample data allow an analysis of electoral participation within the framework of varying political settings. *Gemeinden*, as communities, form the background against which individual behavior occurs. After learning how voters in each community vote as a body, we may generalize about the constellation of characteristics associated with certain types of voting.

1. See Campbell et al., pp. 49–66, 145–46; Lester Milbrath, *Political Participation*, pp. 90–109; V. O. Key, Jr., *Southern Politics*, pp. 510–23; Key, *Politics, Parties, and Pressure Groups*, p. 594; Rokkan and Valen, "The Mobilization of the Periphery," pp. 183–99; and Rokkan, "Electoral Mobilization," p. 261.
2. Kesselman, pp. 17–30; Tarrow, "The Urban-Rural Cleavage," pp. 343–46.

The aggregate turnout data discussed in chapter 3 demonstrated general tendencies, but the characteristics of small *Gemeinden*, the overwhelming majority, were masked through the presence of a few large cities. The trends discussed below reflect primarily the patterns of voting turnout in *Gemeinden* of 10,000 and fewer inhabitants. These small units account for 99 per cent of the *Gemeinden* and for 66 per cent of the electorate.

Using the sample data based on the *Gemeinde* as the data unit, we find that national and local turnout discrepancies are minimized. The specific breakdown of local, national, and state turnout rates is given in Table 20. In each election during the period under observation,

TABLE 20
TURNOUT DISCREPANCIES IN NATIONAL,
STATE, AND LOCAL ELECTIONS[a]
(in percentages)

Election Years			Average Local Turnout	Turnout Difference		
State	Local	Nat'l		Nat'l-Local	State-Local	Nat'l-State
1951	1952	1953	81.9	+2.9	− 9.9	+12.8
1955	1956	1957	82.5	+5.5	− 7.9	+13.4
1959	1960	1961	83.7	+4.2	− 6.6	+10.8
1963	1964	1965	85.5	+1.7	−10.0	+11.7

a. Difference of means test significant at .001 level.

electoral participation increased in local elections. National turnout, however, remained stable at approximately 88 per cent after the 1957 election. A plateau of participation has been reached in national elections which has not been reached in the local elections.[3] Thus, in the most recent local and national elections, the difference in turnout was less than 2 per cent. Voter turnout in local elections is not greatly distinguished from voter turnout in national elections.[4] State elections, by contrast, mobilize significantly fewer voters than do either local or

3. This "leveling off" of turnout rates in national elections is characteristic of the Federal Republic as a whole. The turnout percentages for each national election are: 1949, 78.5; 1953, 85.8; 1957, 87.8; 1961, 87.7; 1965, 86.8; 1969, 86.7.
4. Of comparative interest are findings in other European countries. Analyses of local-national turnout discrepancies in Norwegian communes reveal that turnout is consistently lower in local elections than in national elections. See Rokkan and Valen, "The Mobilization of the Periphery," pp. 184–85. An

national elections. Changes in state election turnout rates have clearly not occurred in proportion to the other changes; turnout stabilized at approximately 76 per cent.

Although voting may represent only minimal involvement in the political process, this involvement clearly varies among levels of the political system.[5] That fewer citizens vote in state than in national elections has long been observed in Germany and other countries. A common explanation is that turnout in national elections is higher than in state elections because the less committed partisans vote in national elections, whereas only "core" party supporters participate in state elections.[6] Participation is thus to some degree a result of interest aroused largely by political party appeals. If partisan mobilization is a key to electoral activeness, local elections, which are overwhelmingly nonpartisan, should show the lowest turnout rates of all elections. Yet many more citizens exercise their voting privilege in local than in state elections. In the case of local politics, local identity and social pressures replace partisanship as the motivating factor.

THE FUNCTION OF SIZE

Gemeinden with 10,000 and fewer inhabitants show different turnout tendencies from the *Gemeinden* with 10,000 and more inhabitants. The relevance of size is demonstrated in Table 21, where *Gemeinden* are stratified into small and large units.[7] Size of commune is inversely related to turnout rates in local elections. A great discrepancy is present in the local contests, occasioned by a sharp drop of 8.5 per cent in the large communes. The national-local differences in turnout rates are more marked in the large units than in the small because of the

---

average of 3 per cent more Frenchmen vote in local elections than in national elections. See Kesselman, p. 23.

5. For a discussion of citizen participation in Germany, see Verba, pp. 146–54, and Franz Urban Pappi, *Wahlverhalten und Politische Kultur.*

6. See Heidenheimer, *The Governments of Germany*, p. 202.

7. The number of large cities in our sample was inadequate for comparative purposes. The statistical analyses reported in official election publications were used for these calculations. The selection of the years analyzed was dictated by the availability of information on turnout by size of *Gemeinde*. Likewise, the size stratification of *Gemeinden* into those of fewer than and more than 10,000 inhabitants was necessitated by a lack of other comparative stratification schemes used in national and local election reports.

small local turnout there. National turnout, in contrast, shows scarcely any differentiation according to the size of the *Gemeinde*. The relation of town size to turnout varies cross-nationally. Norwegian cities have higher local and national turnout rates than do rural communes, and the greatest local-national turnout discrepancies occur in the rural communes.[8] Turnout patterns in French communes are the opposite of Norwegian patterns. Turnout varies directly with communal size.[9] German electoral participation is quite similar to French in both its higher local turnout rates and the inverse relationship of size to local turnout.

TABLE 21
TURNOUT RATES BY SIZE OF *Gemeinde*[a]
(in percentages)

Election	*Gemeinden* with Fewer than 10,000 Inhabitants	*Gemeinden* with More than 10,000 Inhabitants
1960 local	83.7	75.2
1961 national	87.2	86.5

a. Calculations based upon the *Gemeinde* as the data unit. Total *Gemeinden*, 2,916.

The structural characteristics of small units encourage more active participation in local elections. There exists a high proportion of local offices to local citizens, and the campaigns are highly personalistic. One votes for or against a person—most likely his neighbor or a relative—and not just a name on the ballot. The directness of local campaigning is lost as the unit becomes larger, and voter solicitation may become less intense.[10]

However, among *Gemeinden* of fewer than 10,000 inhabitants, size loses its explanatory value. For instance, in 1964, communes of under 150 inhabitants showed the highest turnout rates—88.5 per cent; but beyond this size, no direct relationship was observed. The Pearson product-moment correlation coefficient of population size and voter

8. Rokkan and Valen, "The Mobilization of the Periphery," pp. 184–85.
9. Kesselman, p. 25.
10. For a discussion of how the political ecology of small communes encourages high participation, see Tarrow, "The Urban-Rural Cleavage," p. 356. Cf. Rokkan, "Citizen Participation in Political Life," p. 376, and Key, *Southern Politics*, pp. 510–13.

turnout in the 1964 local election showed a statistically significant but very weak negative relationship (−.14). Thus, while size of a political unit may help to account for turnout variations between gross categories of *Gemeinden*, it does not influence electoral participation in a consistent linear fashion. To determine sources of variation in local turnout rates, we now turn to a consideration of communal political features.

THE ELECTORAL SYSTEM

Mean turnout percentages were calculated for local elections between 1952 and 1964 according to the type of electoral contest. In agreement with Norwegian communal research, we found that communes with noncompetitive, plurality elections had statistically significant lower electoral participation than did the communes holding competitive PR elections.[11] These differences, while statistically significant, must be greatly qualified for German electorates. They apply only for the last three elections, and they are small. In contrast to the German communes, Norwegian communes with PR elections mobilized from 13 per cent to 20 per cent more voters than did the communes with plurality elections in the period 1945–59.[12] In the German local elections of 1952, plurality and PR elections reflected no significant differences in turnout rates. These small communes with plurality elections still show higher turnout rates in all local elections than their urban counterparts with PR competitive elections. The differences in voter participation for the sample *Gemeinden* by type of electoral system are given in Table 22.

The lower mean turnout rates in plurality elections belie to some extent the tremendously high interest that is present in many of these contests. In every election some of these communes had 100 per cent voter participation; this full mobilization was not obtained in the PR elections. On the other hand, other communes with plurality electoral systems attracted less than 50 per cent participation. Communes with plurality elections, thus, show the greatest fluctuations in voter turnout. The standard deviation of turnout in plurality elections stood at a

11. Cf. Rokkan and Valen, "The Mobilization of the Periphery," pp. 193–94.
12. Ibid.

mean of 10.51 for the four election years, compared with a mean of 8.38 for the PR elections.

NONPARTISAN AND PARTISAN ELECTIONS

So far we have compared turnout in the units at one extreme with the aggregated turnout for all other units. It is, therefore, of interest to analyze differences in turnout among the PR elections from one level of politicization to another. Of particular concern is the relevance of party incentives for voter mobilization.

TABLE 22
TURNOUT RATES IN PLURALITY AND PR LOCAL ELECTIONS
(in percentages)

Year	Plurality		PR	
	Mean	Standard Deviation	Mean	Standard Deviation
1952	81.9[a]	11.55	82.0[a]	9.93
1956	80.8	10.17	84.1	7.96
1960	82.7	10.75	84.7	7.64
1964	84.8	9.58	86.8	7.97

a. Difference of means test not significant for a one-tailed test; $z = .11$; all other differences are significant at the .05 level.

We first analyzed the PR elections according to the presence or absence of political parties. Whereas nonpartisan PR elections (local voter groups only) showed statistically significant lower turnout rates than partisan PR elections (one or more political parties) in 1952, no significant differences were present between the elections in 1956. By 1960, however, communes with nonpartisan PR elections had a statistically significant higher turnout rate.

Interest in local elections may be becoming more closely associated with the effectiveness of local voter groups. The communes where local voter groups either monopolized the ballot or were present along with only one political party had the highest electoral participation in all elections. A consideration of voting strength revealed that voter turnout was higher in the 1964 elections where local voter groups obtained a majority of the vote against one and more political parties than vice versa.

To evaluate the relevance of local voter groups as opposed to political parties in PR elections, we then excluded the intermediate levels of politicized contests. The communes with solely local voter group list alternatives were compared to the communes with solely party list alternatives (Table 23).

In the first three elections, less than 1 per cent variation in turnout occurred between communes having nonpartisan and fully politicized contests; but by 1964, communes having only local voter groups had a statistically significant higher turnout than those communes having only parties. The attractive power of local voter groups is reflected in their average increase of 2.5 per cent in each successive election. In 1964, these *Gemeinden* attained a local turnout of 88.5 per cent of

TABLE 23
DIFFERENCE IN TURNOUT BY *Gemeinden* WITH NONPARTISAN PR
ELECTIONS AND WITH SOLELY PARTISAN PR ELECTIONS
(in percentages)

Year	Nonpartisan Elections	Solely Partisan Elections
1952	80.8	80.3
1956	83.3	83.0
1960	85.9	85.5
1964	88.5[a]	85.6[a]

a. Difference of means test significant at the .05 level for a one-tailed test.

the electorate. *Gemeinden* monopolized electorally by parties, in contrast, rose to a high of approximately 85 per cent in 1960 and remained at that level in 1964. We might infer that the reservoir of voters for partisan factions is not as great as for local voter groups, since more of the electorate was consistently mobilized in each nonpartisan election.

From additional investigations, there is some basis for hypothesizing that purely partisan electoral politics actually retard local involvement. An analysis was made of changes in electoral list alternatives in successive elections with respect to the inclusion or exclusion of local voter groups. Voter turnout declined in each pair of elections analyzed in the communes in which exclusion replaced inclusion. On the other hand, turnout rates increased in the communes which "reverted" from purely partisan elections to allow the inclusion of local voter groups.[13]

13. Turnout differences for *Gemeinden* exhibiting electoral list changes were computed relative to those turnout differences for *Gemeinden* not exhibiting electoral list changes.

The relationship of nonpartisan and partisan elections to high turn-out may be evaluated from another point of view. Over one-third of the communes actually had greater turnout for the 1964 local elections than for the 1965 national elections. Their mean turnout in 1964 was a very high 89.8 per cent. These large turnout rates showed an inverse relationship to the presence of political parties. The mean index of partisan mobilization (6.6) demonstrates the extreme electoral weakness of political parties in communes with very high local participation.[14] With each step toward full politicization, high local turnout became rarer. Table 24 gives the percentage of *Gemeinden* at each level of politicization with greater participation in the local than in the national elections.

TABLE 24
Gemeinden WITH 1964 LOCAL TURNOUT GREATER THAN 1965
NATIONAL TURNOUT BY LEVEL OF POLITICIZATION
(in percentages)

1 or no list, plurality election	40.7
Local voter group lists only	46.7
1 party list, 1 or more local voter group lists	39.1
2 or more party lists, 1 or more local voter group lists	9.1
Political party lists only	5.3

More than two-fifths of all *Gemeinden* with nonpartisan local elections (plurality, or PR with local voter groups only) had more participation on the local than on the national level, compared with a mere 5 per cent of all *Gemeinden* with purely partisan elections. Clearly, nonpartisan elections do not lead to voter apathy, nor do partisan cleavages activate greater interest in local electorates. On the contrary, the reverse appears to be true.

On the other hand, the importance of the politicization of local electorates to electoral participation derives from its relationship to national turnout rates. As the level of politicization in local elections rose, so did the turnout in national elections. Between 1952 and 1964, communes with fully politicized local contests mobilized an average of 4.5 per cent more voters in national elections than did communes with nonpartisan local elections. When we evaluated national turnout accord-

14. The method of calculation for the index of partisan mobilization is given in chapter 4, note 12.

ing to the local electoral strength of political parties, however, we found a statistically significant but theoretically insignificant relationship: Pearson product-moment correlation coefficient of the 1964 partisan mobilization index and the 1965 turnout percentage was .18.[15]

Our data analysis causes us to question the view that political parties are the primary agents of integration and mobilization at the local level. Local notables and local voter groups equal and often surpass the parties as such agents. Communal factors that encourage high electoral involvement may, in fact, retard partisan involvement. For example, when parties are viewed as precursors of open political conflict and personal strife, the penetration of the party system into new territory is resisted. Small-town dwellers synthesize high voter turnout with predominantly noncompetitive or nonpartisan elections, suggesting that voting is a culturally accepted community norm whereas local party organizations are not. Electorates do not necessarily mobilize in a partisan direction.

If mobilization toward participation in the electoral process and partisan mobilization are quite distinct phenomena, the possibility of change in the character of local elections depends upon the direction of change in voters' perceptions rather than the extent of change in their participation. No new influx of voters exists for activation by the parties, since so many already participate. High voter turnout occurs independently of partisan mobilization. The extension of the party system to encompass local electorates cannot be achieved, therefore, through increased voter turnout.

Our research suggests a corollary to the generalizations about the linkage of party system development with electoral participation. Most of the Western mass parties emerged with the extension of suffrage to new groups of citizens. The origins of political parties have thus caused them to be associated with the idea that political power must include participation by the mass public.[16] Yet the local weakness of German and French parties exists where universal suffrage has long been present and high voter turnout long achieved. The expansion of mass participation on the local level is not necessarily accompanied by a corresponding spread of the party system.

15. Cf. the Norwegian findings reported in Rokkan and Valen, "The Mobilization of the Periphery," p. 195.

16. Joseph LaPalombara and Myron Weiner, "The Origin and Development of Political Parties," pp. 3–42. Cf. Seymour M. Lipset and Stein Rokkan, "Cleavage Structures, Party Systems, and Voter Alignments: An Introduction."

6. National Parties and Their Local Electorates

THE party system exists largely on top of communal politics. The process of politicization is still in the elementary stages. Party conflict has spread to encompass a mere one-fourth of the local electorates, and local voter groups exist alongside political parties in most of these cases.

How the vote is structured in this minority of *Gemeinden* into which national party organizations have penetrated is the focus of this chapter. We wish to examine changes in the structure and character of the local party system. How well do parties fare against one another and against local voter groups? What sources of strength exist for the various electoral competitors? What direction does change in voting patterns assume? How are parties and local voter groups tied in with the communal socioeconomic structure?

THE PATTERN OF PARTY DEVELOPMENT

The battle for partisan mobilization is fought among three partisan contestants, the CDU, the SPD, and the FDP, against numerous local voter groups. Of interest is the pattern of development of the national parties in establishing local organizations. Does a particular party initially mobilize local electorates and do other parties enter later after the barriers to partisan mobilization have been lowered, or do several parties simultaneously penetrate new territory? In determining which parties first entered local elections, we considered the *Gemeinden* which had only one political party in opposition to one or more local voter groups. Table 25 shows the composition of the party lists in these communes.

When only one party competes in local elections, it is likely to be the CDU, yet SPD local organizations are far from negligible, since they are present in two-fifths of these *Gemeinden*. The FDP, by contrast, does not enter actively into communal politics as the sole partisan agent.

The efforts of the CDU to mobilize supporters initially in local elections may be linked to the nature of the communes at this stage of politicization. Partisan politics first makes its entry in small towns of 500–3,000 inhabitants.[1] The strength of the CDU in the rural areas and small towns of the Federal Republic has long been affirmed in national findings.[2] That the CDU is a significant force of partisan penetration may be related, then, to the availability of local supporters in these communes. The SPD, as a largely urban party, seemingly has fewer incentives to compete in the very small towns.

TABLE 25
FIRST PARTY TO ENTER LOCAL ELECTIONS[a]

Party	1952		1956		1960		1964	
	no.	%	no.	%	no.	%	no.	%
CDU	42	51.9	39	56.5	35	57.4	37	53.6
SPD	37	45.7	30	43.5	25	41.0	31	44.9
FDP	1	1.2	0	0.0	1	1.6	1	1.4
Other	1	1.2	0	0.0	0	0.0	0	0.0
Total	81	100.0	69	100.0	61	100.0	69	99.9[b]

a. In *Gemeinden* with one party list and one or more local voter group lists.
b. Rounding error.

However, in each successive election, the SPD has scored greater gains over the CDU in its ability to penetrate new territory. We analyzed those communes which changed from plurality or PR elections with only local voter groups to include one political party. Of the fifteen *Gemeinden* which so changed between 1952 and 1956, the SPD was the political party in only three cases. By 1964, the SPD was the sole party in twelve cases and the CDU in fifteen cases where no party had been present in the 1960 election. The commanding lead held by the CDU in first mobilizing local partisans is diminishing. The CDU maintains its superior position, however, since very few communes change to partisan elections.

In the total number of partisan elections contested, the CDU continues to hold a slight advantage over the SPD.[3] Table 26 shows the

1. Cf. Table 15.
2. See the studies cited in chapter 1, note 14.
3. The aggregate statistics indicate that in 1969 the SPD entered more local elections than did the CDU.

proportion of contesting parties and local voter groups in all partisan elections. The most active partisan competitor, the CDU, has made the most dramatic increases in entering local contests, so that in 1960 it presented candidates in 80 per cent of the partisan elections. The SPD has local units organized in three-fourths of the partisan communes, while the FDP is a minor local contestant entering less than one-fifth of these elections.

TABLE 26
PROPORTION OF PARTISAN LOCAL ELECTIONS CONTESTED
BY PARTIES AND LOCAL VOTER GROUPS

Contestant	1952 (N=157)		1956 (N=140)		1960 (N=142)		1964 (N=154)	
	no.	%	no.	%	no.	%	no.	%
CDU	112	71.3	108	77.1	114	80.3	122	79.2
SPD	110	70.1	100	71.4	106	74.6	115	74.7
FDP	16	10.2	15	10.7	23	16.2	27	17.3
Local voter groups	143	91.1	129	92.1	123	86.6	135	87.7

Local voter groups appear on the ballot in almost all communes. *Gemeinden* with partisan elections rarely succeed in excluding local groups, but partisan elections do show slight indications of becoming more politicized. A consideration of changes in the number of party lists presented in an election suggests that local partisan agents have become entrenched. The presence of only one party contender was characteristic of 52 per cent of all partisan elections in 1952. The proportion dropped to 45 per cent in 1964 because of increases in the number of partisan elections with two or more party lists (from 40 per cent in 1952 to 43 per cent in 1964), and because of increases in purely partisan list alternatives (from 9 per cent in 1952 to 12 per cent in 1964).

THE ELECTORAL STRENGTH OF PARTIES

To evaluate further how parties and local voter groups fare in local elections, we must consider their voting strength. Table 27 gives the percentage of the total partisan vote obtained by each competitor.

Local voter groups, the most active contestants, also won the plurality of votes. Although they showed a slight decline in voting strength over the four elections, they held the lead steadfastly over the individual partisan opponents. The CDU and SPD each received approximately three-tenths of the vote in 1964, and the SPD has more consistently bettered its position than has the CDU.[4] The FDP remained an insignificant contestant in terms of voting strength as well as presence.

Sharp differences in the voting strength of parties are apparent, though, among the three types of partisan elections according to electoral list alternatives. For instance, the CDU makes a better electoral

TABLE 27
PROPORTION OF VOTE OBTAINED BY POLITICAL PARTIES AND LOCAL
VOTER GROUPS IN LOCAL PARTISAN ELECTIONS
(in percentages)

Contestant	1952	1956	1960	1964
CDU	29.8	29.8	32.2	31.4
SPD	25.0	26.3	26.4	27.7
FDP	2.0	1.7	2.4	2.8
Other parties	1.6	0.3	0.1	0.0
Local voter groups	41.5	40.1	38.8	38.2
	99.9[a]	98.2[b]	99.9[a]	100.1[a]

a. Rounding error.
b. Error in statistical information or in data preparation for computer processing.

showing against local voter groups than does the SPD. When the CDU was the sole partisan opponent against local voter groups, the difference between CDU and local voter groups votes was a mean 5.6 per cent for 1952–64. The CDU received a majority of the vote in the first two elections, and the local voter groups received a majority of the vote in the second two elections. The mean difference in vote for SPD and local voter groups was 20.5 per cent for 1952–64. Local voter groups were the recipients of the majority vote in each election. Since Rhineland-Palatinate is a "CDU state," we cannot assume de facto that the CDU is a stronger competitor against local voter groups

4. The aggregate statistics show that the SPD has received more votes than the CDU from 1956 onwards. This divergence from our sample data stems from the high percentage of votes received by the SPD in large cities. In 1964, the SPD obtained an absolute majority of the vote in seven of the twelve *kreisfrei* cities of Rhineland-Palatinate.

than is the SPD. Comparable research in predominantly "SPD states" would indicate the extent of any linkage between state and local strength.

Table 28 presents the dispersion of the votes of party and local voter groups by the character of the electoral list alternatives. Local

TABLE 28
DIFFERENCES IN PARTISAN VOTING STRENGTH BETWEEN "LESS
POLITICIZED" AND "MORE POLITICIZED" COMMUNES
(in percentages)

Contestant	1952	1956	1960	1964
1 party list, 1 or more local voter group lists				
CDU	26.9	28.5	26.2	25.6
SPD	19.6	17.2	16.7	15.9
FDP	0.6[a]	0.0	0.1	1.7
Local voter groups	52.9	51.2	56.9	56.9
	100.0	96.9[b]	99.9[c]	100.1[c]
	N=81	N=69	N=61	N=69
2 or more party lists, 1 or more local voter group lists				
CDU	28.5	27.8	33.7	33.6
SPD	29.8	34.0	30.1	34.3
FDP	2.4	2.3	3.1	2.6
Other parties	3.1	0.6	0.3	0.0
Local voter groups	36.1	34.6	32.8	29.6
	99.9[c]	99.3[b]	100.0	100.1[c]
	N=62	N=60	N=62	N=66
Party lists only				
CDU	52.3	49.4	46.8	45.1
SPD	34.8	41.9	45.4	47.3
FDP	10.5	8.6	7.8	7.6
Other parties	2.3	0.0	0.0	0.0
	99.9[c]	99.9[c]	100.0	100.0
	N=14	N=11	N=19	N=19

a. Includes a small proportion of "other party" votes.
b. Error in statistical information or in data preparation for computer processing.
c. Rounding error.

voter groups steadily obtained a majority of the votes against one-party contenders in the 1952–64 elections. The decrease in their percentage of total votes (see Table 27) derived from their changes in strength against two or more political parties. In the 1960s, the local voter groups were surpassed by political parties and lost the plurality of votes they had held in the 1950s.

The CDU's lead over the SPD in partisan votes comes from the large proportion of votes obtained in contests where it is the lone partisan contestant in opposition to local voter groups. In elections with two or more parties, the CDU fares less well than does the SPD. The CDU in purely partisan elections originally obtained a majority of the votes, but gradually declined while the SPD was leaping forward. The SPD gains enabled it to surpass the CDU in the 1964 elections. The SPD, in terms of voting strength, is a weak competitor against local voter groups. Against other parties, the SPD has shown the largest increases. The FDP is very weak against partisan and nonpartisan opponents alike.

The CDU, the SPD, and local voter groups each have sources of strength in a core of communes. While the CDU and the SPD have achieved close parity with each other, neither can equal the attractive power of local voter groups. In 1964, the CDU received a plurality or majority of the votes in 31.8 per cent of the 154 sample *Gemeinden* holding some form of partisan elections. The SPD was close behind the CDU in dominating 30.5 per cent of the elections, while the local voter groups monopolized 37.7 per cent of these elections. The mean winning vote of local voter groups, a high 65 per cent, points up once again the endurance and strength of nonpartisan competitors in electoral struggles against agents of partisan mobilization.[5]

Having been grouped according to which party received a plurality or majority of the votes, the communes were then analyzed as to their socioeconomic structure. The sources of strength of the CDU, SPD, and local voter groups in partisan elections are quite different (Table 29).

Local voter groups are strongest in small and sparsely inhabited communes possessing fewer indicators of urbanization and industrialization than do the other communes. The partisan communes dominated by local voter groups are more advanced economically than the communes with no partisan competition, but generally below the means for partisan contests.[6] The CDU communes resemble the local voter group communes in many economic characteristics, but diverge sharply on religion. Catholicism prevails overwhelmingly in the CDU

5. The CDU obtained an absolute majority of the vote in 69.4 per cent of the elections where it surpassed the other opponents. The respective figures for the SPD and local voter groups are 59.6 per cent and 93.1 per cent.
6. Cf. Table 16.

strongholds. An SPD winning vote is, in contrast, quite negatively associated with the percentage of Catholics in a *Gemeinde*. SPD communes, in addition, are the most economically developed. To ascertain the strength of the relationships between a certain type of vote and certain communal structural characteristics, we utilized a series of bi- and multivariate statistical techniques.

TABLE 29
SOCIOECONOMIC STRUCTURE OF COMMUNES BY
"WINNER" OF 1964 LOCAL ELECTIONS[a]

	CDU Communes	SPD Communes	Local Voter Group Communes
Population size	2,040	5,637	1,112
Population density	212	378	154
% self-employed	17.8	15.6	18.5
% white collar workers and civil servants	17.0	19.8	13.8
% manual workers	40.6	45.2	41.2
% female employees	39.3	35.8	38.8
% *Auspendler*	39.7	43.4	44.0
% *Einpendler*	17.8	22.9	13.5
% in agriculture	27.9	19.9	34.0
% in production	39.8	48.0	38.6
% in trade	14.3	16.2	12.8
% in services	18.0	16.0	14.7
% Catholic	88.6	34.4	58.3
% refugees	8.8	12.0	8.6
Community tax strength (DM per inhabitant)	83.6	92.4	65.8

a. Socioeconomic variables are calculated from the 1961 census data; these variables represent means.

LOCAL VOTER GROUPS

The electoral strength of local voter groups, as was expected, was inversely related to the main socioeconomic correlates of the index of partisan mobilization.[7] The simple correlation coefficient of 1964 local voter group vote with percentage of white collar workers and civil servants in a commune was −.50, and with population density −.47.[8]

7. Cf. Table 17.
8. Correlation coefficients were calculated only for those PR elections in which local voter groups were on the ballot. These correlations are significant at the .001 level.

Weaker negative correlations existed with the other indicators of socio-economic development as well.

Not surprisingly, the importance of ruralism for support of local voter groups emerges quite clearly when we note the simple correlation coefficients of three of its indicators: .46 with percentage of population in agriculture, .31 with percentage of self-employed workers, and .27 with percentage of female workers.

To evaluate the cumulative effect of the demographic variables upon local voter group strength, we next employed multiple stepwise regression analysis. The findings are reported in Table 30.

TABLE 30
MULTIPLE STEPWISE REGRESSION OF LOCAL VOTER
GROUP VOTE IN 1964 LOCAL ELECTIONS[a]

Independent Variables	Multiple R	Variance Accounted For
White collar workers and civil servants	.498	.248
Population density	.532	.283
Catholics	.542	.294
Production	.556	.310
Municipal streets	.564	.321

a. The independent variables are calculated from 1961 census data. The correlations are reported only for those variables whose individual contribution to R^2 was greater than 1 per cent. All correlations are significant at the .01 level.

The total contribution of five demographic variables accounts for one-third of the variance in the votes of local voter groups. It is of interest that the simple *r*'s for all variables are negative. Population density and the proportion of the work force in white collar and civil service occupations, measures of a tertiary economy and urbanization, have the greatest explanatory value. The presence of the Catholic variable supports the implications suggested in Table 29. A commune with a predominance of Catholics, regardless of economic development, was less inclined to vote for nonpartisan groups when the CDU was present.

An additional insight into the relative impact of the demographic variables upon the local voter group vote is provided in a consideration of the changes that took place in the composition of the multiple R between the 1960 and 1964 elections. In 1960, the first step in the multiple stepwise regression analysis was percentage in agriculture with a multiple R of .526, the second step yielded a multiple R of .584 for population density, and the third step showed a multiple R of .590 for percentage in white collar work and civil service. These three variables "explained" 35 per cent of the variance of local voter group vote in 1960. Other variables, while statistically significant, possessed negligible explanatory value.

The 1964 increase in the contributory power of the white collar variable is quite notable. In its explanatory power, the density variable, by contrast, declined, although it remained as the second most important component of the vote of local groups. The main predictor of the local voter group electoral showing in 1960 (percentage in agriculture) did not enter into the later stepwise regression analysis, so that all the independent variables were negatively associated with the dependent variable in 1964.

The movement toward economic modernity and urban life cuts deeply into the ability of local voter groups to compete effectively in local elections. Yet as is the case with partisan mobilization, the type of socioeconomic growth common to communal change is more weakly associated with the electoral position of local voter groups. The contribution to R^2 of the variable measuring the percentage of work force in production was only 1.6 per cent in 1964. Increasing communal social and economic diversity does not necessarily foreshadow the disappearance of local voter groups. In fact, if judged by their overall presence and strength in local elections, local voter groups have more successfully adapted to changing socioeconomic conditions than have the political parties.

A comprehensive examination of the relationship of the demographic variables to voter support for the individual political parties may better illuminate their plight on the local level.[9] A knowledge of the national supporters of the CDU and SPD is inadequate to explain local party support. In national and state elections, the CDU has been predominant in rural Catholic constituencies. This linkage between party strength and religious and social affiliation is not so direct in communal politics.

The first difficulty arises from the classification schemes applied in national research. The criterion of population density is commonly

9. The FDP is such a minor contestant that it is not considered in the following analyses. It competed in a mere 2.7 per cent of our 576 sample *Gemeinden* in 1964 and received a mean 1.2 per cent of the votes in PR elections.

used for differentiating between urban and rural. For example, a constituency is classified as rural if the number of inhabitants per square kilometer is under 400, or alternatively, if 12 per cent or more of the population is engaged in agricultural production.[10] The religious composition of a constituency is determined simply by whether the number of Catholics is greater than the number of Protestants or vice versa, and, in stricter terms, by whether one religion characterizes 60 per cent of the population.[11] By these criteria, our sample *Gemeinden* would be considered rural Catholic constituencies. For the partisan communes, mean density equals 241 inhabitants per square kilometer with a standard deviation of 226; the mean percentage in agriculture equals 28, standard deviation, 18; and the mean population is 61 per cent Catholic with a standard deviation of 35. A classification scheme in which such an overwhelming proportion of cases fall into one category is useless.

The second difficulty arises from the nature of the conclusions drawn from the association of demographic variables to CDU and SPD strength. From the information derived from national research, we would have predicted that the CDU would be quite strong in local elections, and that the SPD would, correspondingly, be very weak. Yet our research showed that the CDU and the SPD were almost equal in both electoral presence and voting strength in local elections. Most important, the CDU has been unable to mobilize its reservoir of traditional supporters. Local CDU electoral forces existed in only 662 of the 2,918 *Gemeinden* and obtained 26 per cent of the total votes cast in 1964.

In the following discussions, the reader should remember the differences inherent in using a *Gemeinde* instead of a federal voting district as the data unit. There were 23,629 *Gemeinden* in the Federal Republic at the time of this data collection, but only 248 federal voting districts. A description in terms of the composition of the voting district severely masks the variations among individual municipalities.[12] Ur-

10. Klingemann and Pappi utilize the density criterion, while Kaase applies the agricultural criterion.

11. These classifications are used by Klingemann and Pappi and by Conradt, respectively.

12. The minimizing of extreme variation through data aggregation for large areas falsely inflates the results of most statistical tests. For a discussion of the impact that the unit of aggregation has upon the reliability of such tests, see Erwin K. Scheuch, "Cross-National Comparisons Using Aggregate Data: Some Substantive and Methodological Problems," pp. 131–67.

banism and ruralism and Catholicism and Protestantism are not dichotomous attributes of voting constituencies, but rather they represent segments on a scale. The way these features are combined varies in proportion to the size of the unit of analysis. When we use the terms *urban* or *Catholic*, for instance, to describe municipal structural features, we mean merely that the *Gemeinden* to which we refer possess more indicators of urbanism or Catholicism than other *Gemeinden* possess.

THE CHRISTIAN DEMOCRATS

Our 1961 census data allowed an analysis of the interrelationships of social structure and voting behavior for the 1956–64 elections. The Pearson product-moment correlation coefficients for the independent variables with CDU vote are given in Table 31.[13] The CDU vote has remained most closely and steadily linked to the Catholic variable, and its ability to explain the variance in CDU vote has increased in each election from 29 per cent in the 1956 election to 42 per cent in 1964. The second of the variables which best account for the Christian Democrat variance is the proportion of refugees in a *Gemeinde*.[14] The other correlations in Table 31 are most notable for their lack of explanatory power; all economic variables are weakly associated with the CDU poll.

The importance of these independent variables lies in the nature of their association with the Christian Democratic poll. All indicators of economic and social growth are negatively related. Ominously, the magnitude of this negativism has generally increased over the three elections. Each of the positively related economic correlations to CDU vote reflects agrarianism: proportions of the population in agriculture, of small farms, and of female employees. CDU strength is clearly confined to the stagnant sectors of the economy.

In this respect, it should be noted that agriculture was a stronger source for local voter groups ($r = .46$) than for the CDU ($r = .20$)

13. Cf. the demographic correlates of CDU vote in the 1965 national and 1963 state elections, Appendix E. These correlations are also based upon the *Gemeinde* as the data unit.

14. The intercorrelation matrix of the demographic variables reveals that the refugee variable is more closely related to the Catholic variable than any other; however, the strength of the relationship is weak: $r = .24$.

TABLE 31
MAIN DEMOGRAPHIC CORRELATES OF LOCAL
CDU VOTE BY *Gemeinde*, 1956–64[a]

Sociostructural Variables	Correlation to CDU Vote		
	1956	1960	1964
Population size	−.20	−.16	−.15
Population density	−.21	−.15*	−.17
Change in population, 1950–61	−.06*	−.06*	−.21
Catholics	.54	.58	.65
Refugees	−.22	−.28	−.29
Agriculture	.21	.14*	.20
Small farms[b]	.23	.19	.19
Production	−.06*	−.11*	−.17
Trade	−.27	−.13*	−.21
Female employees	.14*	.11*	.26
White collar workers and civil servants	−.24	−.08*	−.21
Manual workers	−.03*	−.14*	−.15

a. The demographic variables are calculated from 1961 census data. The data units are the *Gemeinden* where a CDU list appeared on the ballot in PR elections: 1956 N = 108, 1960 N = 114, and 1964 N = 122. All of the simple correlation coefficients are significant at at least the .05 level except those marked with an asterisk.
b. Percentage of farms under 7.5 hectares.

in 1964. That agriculture is of little help to the CDU locally is obvious from analyses of the party's change indexes for 1956–60 and 1960–64.[15] The change indexes indicated that the CDU in the second election of each pair lost votes in relation to its previous poll. The correlations of percentage agriculture were −.30 with the 1956–60 change index and −.24 with the 1960–64 change index: the agriculture variable increased the losses of the CDU.[16] In contrast, the correlations of the percentage in agriculture with the change indexes of local voter groups indicated that agriculture inhibited local voter group losses in 1956–60 and 1960–64. The Christian Democrats, on the

15. The formula for calculating the 1960–64 CDU change index was:
$$I = \frac{\text{Percentage of CDU vote, 1964}}{\text{Percentage of CDU vote, 1960}} \cdot 100$$
where CDU vote in 1960 was greater than zero. Index values less than 100 indicate party losses; values greater than 100 indicate party gains. Cf. the similar change indexes employed by Hirsch-Weber and Schuetz, pp. 434–41.
16. These simple correlation coefficients are significant at the .001 level and the .01 level respectively.

local level of the electoral system, have no significant bases of support, with the exception of Catholicism.

Our multivariate analysis tends to confirm this observation. Table 32 gives the results of a multiple stepwise regression of the demographic variables upon the CDU vote in 1964. Signifying the inability of other economic and social factors to come anywhere close to the import of Catholicism, the cumulative contribution of six additional demographic variables yielded an increase in R^2 of only 11.6 per cent.

TABLE 32
MULTIPLE STEPWISE REGRESSION
OF LOCAL CDU VOTE IN 1964[a]

Independent Variable	Multiple R	Variance Accounted For
Catholics	.648	.420
Female employees	.659	.434
Self-employed	.678	.460
Change in population, 1950–61	.689	.475
Refugees	.716	.512
Trade	.725	.525
Manual workers	.732	.536

a. The correlates are reported only for those variables whose individual contribution to R^2 was greater than 1 per cent. All correlations are significant at the .001 level. The independent variables are calculated from 1961 census data.

The Pearson product-moment correlations and the multiple stepwise regression analysis indicate that there is no clear-cut economic explanation of the CDU local vote, but the nature of the relationship suggests an intriguing phenomenon. Economic correlates of the CDU vote, albeit weak, are the opposite of the correlates of political fractionalization and partisan mobilization. A certain level of economic development, exemplified by an increase in the industrial sector and a corresponding decrease in the agricultural sector, comes close to being a prerequisite of political fractionalization. At the same time, partisan mobilization succeeds to the greatest extent in those *Gemeinden* exhibiting growth toward a tertiary economy and larger political units. Indicators of both these changes are unfavorable to Christian Democratic electoral strength. Structural conditions which encourage partisan mobilization are simultaneously in conflict with CDU entrenchment. CDU strength rests largely in the least modern sectors of the economy.

THE SOCIAL DEMOCRATS

In our correlational analysis of the other major local party contestant, the SPD, the religious dimension assumed greater relevance over time so that it was the most important structural variable determining party vote in 1964. Table 33 presents the Pearson product-moment correlation coefficients of the demographic variables with the SPD vote from 1956 to 1964.[17]

TABLE 33
MAIN DEMOGRAPHIC CORRELATES OF LOCAL
SPD VOTE BY *Gemeinde*, 1956–64[a]

Sociostructural Variables	Correlation to SPD Vote		
	1956	1960	1964
Population density	.17	.15*	.23
Catholics	−.38	−.48	−.40
Population over 65 years of age	−.22	−.16	−.13*
Refugees	.24	.17	.14*
Small farms[b]	−.31	−.27	−.30
Production	.42	.41	.30
Services	−.21	−.18	−.15*
Auspendler	.27	.31	.12*
Female employees	−.32	−.33	−.28
Self-employed	−.36	−.34	−.28
Manual workers	.42	.36	.23

a. The demographic variables are calculated from 1961 census data. The data units are the *Gemeinden* where a SPD list appeared on the ballot in PR elections: 1956 N = 100, 1960 N = 106, and 1964 N = 115. All of the simple correlation coefficients are significant at at least the .05 level except those marked with an asterisk.
b. Percentage of farms under 7.5 hectares.

In Catholic areas, the SPD is definitely the loser. The SPD's ability to surmount this religious barrier is indicated, however, by a consideration of other communal structural features. The correlates of an industrial economy—proportion of workers in production and in manual occupation—are moderately related to support for the Social Democrats. This positive linkage of the SPD to communal economic conditions is greater than the corresponding positive linkage of the

17. Cf. the demographic correlates of SPD vote in the 1965 national and 1963 state elections, Appendix F. These correlations are also based upon the *Gemeinde* as the data unit.

CDU. Although the impact of these variables upon the SPD poll has lessened over the three elections, this change is mitigated by other factors. The "unattractiveness" of the SPD to a different sector of the economy has lessened as well. Measures of a rural work force—percentage of female employees and self-employed—were not as negatively associated with the SPD vote in 1964 as in 1956.

The success of the Social Democrats in broadening their local appeal shows up dramatically in an examination of the demographic correlates of their change indexes. The SPD improved its electoral position in the 1964 elections in those *Gemeinden* where it had competed in 1960. These increases were positively related to percentage of females ($r = .32$), Catholics ($r = .26$), services ($r = .22$), trade ($r = .22$), and white collar workers and civil servants ($r = .22$).[18] The local SPD made a dent in the CDU strongholds of Catholics at the same time as it capitalized on modern economic settings.

The effects of SPD gains among Catholics, while very limited, are discernible in the 1960 and 1964 multiple stepwise regression analyses presented in Table 34.

TABLE 34
MULTIPLE STEPWISE REGRESSION OF LOCAL
SPD VOTE IN 1960 AND 1964[a]

Year	Independent Variable	Multiple R	Variance Accounted For
1960	Catholics	.484	.235
	Production	.604	.365
	Female employees	.629	.396
	Population over 65 years	.649	.421
	Trade	.656	.431
	Einpendler	.673	.453
1964	Catholics	.402	.162
	Production	.479	.229
	Trade	.516	.267
	Small farms[b]	.533	.284
	Einpendler	.548	.301
	Population density	.566	.320
	Population over 65 years	.575	.330

a. The correlates are reported only for those variables whose individual contribution to R^2 was greater than 1 per cent. All correlations are significant at the .01 level. The independent variables are calculated from 1961 census data.
b. Percentage of farms under 7.5 hectares.

Although Catholicism was the most important single factor accounting for the Social Democrats' poll, its significance declined considerably between 1960 and 1964. At the same time, the economic conditions assumed more relevance. The production variable doubled its contribution to R^2 in the two elections, and the trade variable tripled its contribution.

The electoral position of the SPD, unlike that of the CDU, should benefit from any movement toward political fractionalization and partisan mobilization. In addition, the SPD seems capable of adapting its strategies to conform to the present structural realities of communal politics—a fact indicated by the weakening of negative associations of Catholicism and the agrarian indicators of self-employed and female employees. Although the CDU has been greatly favored by communal socioeconomic features, it is most notable for its inability to capitalize on these structural conditions. CDU failures, in this respect, derive from the successes of its primary opponent, local voter groups.

18. All correlations are significant at the .01 level. In the 1965 national election, SPD increases were also positively associated with Catholicism, $r = .27$.

7. The Development of Party Systems

ELECTORAL politics at the local level shares few similarities with electoral politics at the national level. The primary differences relate to the question "What entities, as the result of their activities, or even of their mere existence, have the effect of structuring the vote?"[1] As we have remarked, on the local level, in contrast to the national, vote-structuring may take place without any parties at all.

What accounts for the preeminence of political parties on the national level and their weakness on the local level? According to one explanation, the party system is the outgrowth of basic socioeconomic change in which political parties are the dependent variables.[2] In this connection, it is helpful to conceptualize a plateau of socioeconomic development which is conducive to partisan mobilization, as was done in chapter 4. While lower levels of socioeconomic development may hinder partisan mobilization on the local level, they may not preclude it. An alternative proposition will now be considered: political variables are the primary factors in the development of a party system. This proposition will be examined through a consideration of the aims of the national party, the electoral behavior of the *Gemeinde* members, the cleavage structure of local politics, and the attitudes of local party officeholders.

THE LOCAL PARTY-VOTE RELATIONSHIP

It is reasonable to assume that a party seeking votes at the national level may see the politicization of local electorates as helpful. By establishing local organizations geared for electoral struggle, the party

1. King, p. 121.
2. See LaPalombara and Weiner, "The Origin and Development of Political Parties," pp. 19–21.

maintains continuity and stability of followers between national elections. Yet our data analysis indicates that the *Gemeinde* is not the most advantageous level on which to expend party efforts. Whereas the state elections percentages of a specific party vote showed almost perfect linear relationships with the following national elections, the local elections percentages of party vote showed an average correlation of .6. Table 35 gives the Pearson product-moment correlation coefficients for each pair of state-national elections and local-national elections by party.

TABLE 35
CORRELATES OF STATE AND LOCAL PARTY VOTE PERCENTAGES
WITH NATIONAL PARTY VOTE PERCENTAGES, 1951–65[a]

Year		Party		Year		Party	
State	National	CDU	SPD	Local	National	CDU	SPD
1951	1953	.98	.95	1952	1953	.69	.71
1955	1957	.97	.93	1956	1957	.66	.70
1959	1961	.98	.88	1960	1961	.63	.69
1963	1965	.98	.90	1964	1965	.68	.61

a. Local-national party correlations were calculated only for those *Gemeinden* in which the party participated in local elections. National party percentages of the vote are those of the second ballot.

State voting patterns account for at least 84 per cent of the variance in the following national vote. Local voting patterns never account for more than 50 per cent of the variance in the following national vote. In that parties realize efforts spent in increasing national electoral vote could better be spent elsewhere, we can assume that political parties themselves to some degree determine the slow pace of local partisan mobilization. In seeking national office, parties have few incentives to penetrate into the local level of the political system. In fact, with respect to the impact on national vote, a party's presence in local elections may be detrimental. Table 36 shows the share of total national electoral votes received by parties of varying local vote classifications.

Not surprisingly, the parties do best nationally in the *Gemeinden* in which they receive a majority of the local vote. But what is of most interest is their patterns in other communes. Where the CDU participates locally but receives less than 50 per cent of the vote, it actually does worse in terms of national vote than in the communes where it does not participate in local politics at all. The SPD, on the other hand, does show average national increases in proportion to its participation in local elections. However, over time the greatest national gains relatively for the SPD have still come from those *Gemeinden* where it does not enter into local politics. This information supports the proposition that political parties are themselves factors in determining partisan penetration—through their recognition of the small returns in terms of national vote.

TABLE 36
MEAN PARTY VOTE IN NATIONAL ELECTIONS BY
LOCAL ELECTORAL STRENGTH, 1953–65[a]

Years	% CDU Vote		% SPD Vote	
	Local	National	Local	National
1952–53[b]				
	0	57.2	0	16.9
	>0<50	55.9	>0<50	30.9
	≥50	78.4	≥50	51.5
1956–57				
	0	58.0	0	20.3
	>0<50	56.6	>0<50	33.5
	≥50	77.5	≥50	50.8
1960–61				
	0	54.8	0	23.7
	>0<50	48.6	>0<50	36.9
	≥50	69.9	≥50	55.1
1964–65				
	0	55.3	0	26.7
	>0<50	50.5	>0<50	38.8
	≥50	71.0	≥50	52.4

a. National party vote percentages represent the second ballot returns.
b. The first election in each pair is the local election.

We again find weak incentives for partisan competition when we confine our attention to the local elections. A review of the nature of CDU and SPD changes over time shows the extent of continuing local resistance to partisan conflict somewhat dramatically. We compared changes in electoral strength of the parties in three successive elections. Table 37 presents the CDU and SPD change indexes for the three pairs of local elections.[3]

3. For the calculation and interpretation of the party change indexes, see chapter 6, note 15.

In only one election did a party, the SPD in 1964, gain in electoral strength over its previous poll. In general, the SPD shows more staying power than the CDU: mean change indexes, 1956–64, are 93.7 and 86.4 respectively. The CDU never increased its mean position in any of the pairs of elections but rather suffered losses. The politicization of local electorates does not lead to gains in party strength. While

TABLE 37
LOCAL CDU AND SPD CHANGE INDEXES

Party	1952–56	1956–60	1960–64
CDU	79.5	91.7	88.1
SPD	91.3	84.7	105.1

systems of local rule may be challenged by party entry, they by no means fade away. The mean change index for local voter groups for the 1956–64 elections was 99. Local voter groups thus exhibit more staying power in partisan elections than do the political parties. The resistance to political parties will be discussed below.

POLITICAL CLEAVAGE AND VOTER ALIGNMENT

Although sociostructural factors point to differing probabilities for the electoral position of partisan contestants, they, too, are less than satisfactory in accounting for electoral change on the local level. The variance unaccounted for by demographic variables in CDU and SPD votes is large: 46 per cent and 67 per cent respectively.[4] In contrast, the structure of party votes on the national level is quite closely linked to communal sociostructural characteristics. Three demographic variables "explain" 86 per cent of the variance in the 1965 CDU vote, and four demographic variables account for 73 per cent of the variance in the 1965 SPD vote.[5]

A further comparison of the simple correlates of party vote at the various electoral levels reveals two important points.[6] 1) The relationship of religious and class cleavages to party vote is very similar at all levels. A cluster of attributes may be associated with the propensity to vote CDU or SPD. 2) The relevance of these societal

4. See Tables 32 and 33.
5. See Appendixes E and F.
6. See Appendixes E and F and Tables 31 and 33.

divisions to party vote is greater in the national and state elections than in local elections. Whereas state and national correlates of party vote are practically alike in strength, these same correlates are generally much weaker indicators of local party vote.[7]

For example, the strongest indicator of party vote is Catholicism. This variable accounts for 70 per cent of the variance in CDU national vote but for only 42 per cent of the variance in CDU local vote. The respective percentages for variance in SPD national and local votes are 52 and 16. Likewise, although indicators of class are less associated with party votes in our sample, the same national-local discrepancies hold. The agricultural variable is twice as important in determining national CDU vote as local. The production variable is one and one-half times stronger in influencing national SPD vote than local. The objective conditions are the same since the data units of analysis are identical, but social divisions are not translated into partisan conflict with the same intensity in national and local party systems. National and state electorates are more polarized than are local electorates.

The crucial problem suggested by the lack of explanatory power at the *Gemeinde* level compared to the national level is the way societal cleavages become translated into political cleavages. In Sartori's words: "As long as we take for granted that cleavages are *reflected in*, not *produced by*, the political system itself, we necessarily neglect to ask to what extent conflicts and cleavages may either be channeled, deflected, and repressed or, vice versa, activated and reinforced, precisely by the operations and operators of the political system."[8] While parties do not determine the number of Catholics, farmers, or manual workers within a *Gemeinde*, the presence of parties at the local level may determine whether or not Catholicism or class divisions become political issues. A *Gemeinde* has the same divisions of socioeconomic groups in all levels of elections. In state and national elections, the nature of these divisions may be crucial; in local elections, they may have very little predictive value. The only *Gemeinde* difference between levels of elections is the complete par-

---

7. The figures used in these comparisons were all aggregated at the *Gemeinde* level; the resulting correlation coefficients are, thus, of the same reliability. See Scheuch, "Cross-National Comparisons," pp. 148–53.

8. Sartori, p. 89.

tisan mobilization at the national and state levels and the relative lack of partisan mobilization at the local level.

To understand these discrepancies, it is helpful to distinguish between two kinds of voter alignment—the functional and the territorial.[9] Alignment along a functional axis is based upon commitment to a social group cross-locally. One votes with other group members whatever their localities, even if he comes into conflict with others in his own communal environment. The territorial form of alignment is based upon commitment to one's locality and its corresponding norms. Internal socioeconomic cleavages are diffused or suppressed in the interest of local consensus. The differences between local party structure and national are related to the comparative importance of functional and territorial loyalties. The national party system exemplifies the functional form of political representation. German cleavage lines run along religious and class lines which cross-cut each other.[10] The territorial form of cleavage alignment, though not unimportant, is of minor relevance in comparison.[11] On the local level of the political system, however, the importance of functional cleavages is reduced. We suspect the reduction of sociostructural explanations in accounting for local party votes derives from the political importance of the *Gemeinde* as a social group, which is not measurable through ecological data. The *Gemeinde*'s strong influence on its members mitigates the influence of traditional social groupings upon the structure of the vote. In other words, voter alignment is influenced by territorial as well as functional cleavages.

The referent structure influencing voting behavior may be any of several social groups: community, class, or church, for example. One example from a recent survey study of "deviant" community voting behavior in national elections may clarify this idea.[12] In some cases commuters, especially skilled workers, voted as did their counterparts

9. See Lipset and Rokkan, "Cleavage Structures," pp. 9–26, for the formulation of these two cleavage dimensions.

10. See Juan Linz, "Cleavage and Consensus in West German Politics: The Early Fifties," pp. 283–321.

11. The Christian Social Union, the Bavarian-based counterpart of the CDU, exemplifies the remnants of historically strong regionalism.

12. Scheuch, "Social Context and Individual Behavior," p. 153. "Deviant" refers to the voting patterns of cities which could not be explained through ecological data.

in metropolitan areas. In other cases, however, commuters voted according to the prevailing pattern of their "bedroom" community. That belonging to a community may become such an important group reference point in national voting behavior signifies that it is probably even more significant in local voting behavior.

In the local political game, political loyalties to social groups give way to a strong sense of the local community as "us" and of the outside divisive forces as "them." The preeminence of territorial cleavages is clearly indicated in the majority of *Gemeinden* which hold no form of partisan elections. In the minority of *Gemeinden* into which national parties have penetrated, the strength of territorial alignment is maintained, by the political perpetuators of local voter groups. Thus, party candidates for local office, irrespective of partisan affiliation, attempt to assure voters that they are community men rising above narrow party interests reflecting functional cleavages.

ATTITUDES OF LOCAL PARTISAN COUNCILORS

The extent to which local party councilors undertake political representation of community interests instead of party interests is exemplified in a recent study.[13] Local officeholders were asked which kind of political representation they practiced. An absolute majority of the interviewees agreed with the statement "A councilman should represent neither his district and his voters, nor his party, nor particular interests, but only the community or county as a whole."[14] The recognition that the *Gemeinde* may be especially qualified for this form of representation is illustrated in the reply of a CDU respondent. "That may be different at higher levels of government. Here your own views are usually in harmony with the general interest, as in the case of new schools. Most questions we deal with are from the beginning directed toward the common good."

The inappropriateness of party politics to communal politics was particularly underlined. A majority of the partisan councilors themselves could not fully support the proposition "A councilman should in the first place represent the interest of his party and work closely with the majority of his party." Those who rejected completely the

---

13. Arthur B. Gunlicks, "Representative Role Perceptions among Local Councilors in Western Germany."
14. Ibid., p. 449. All the quotations cited below are from pp. 449–52.

role of a party man were most vehement in distinguishing the local level from other levels. One respondent said: "No, because party tactical considerations are inappropriate here. They are by nature foreign to our situation. Party politics have no place here." Another respondent replied: "At the local level we deal mostly with technical questions that have nothing to do with party politics." A third answered: "No, I'm of the opinion that one must be free and not act according to party guidelines. Especially not here in the village. That doesn't fit here." These answers came from SPD, CDU, and FDP councilors respectively. Those councilors who expressed conditional approval of the party-man role evinced the same feelings. A CDU council member said: "Not necessarily. Party politics aren't always appropriate here at the local level." An FDP officeholder replied: "He must see whether or not the party line is advantageous for his level, however. With this limitation, yes." Another FDP member said: "Not as the main goal. Party views must be coordinated with voter interests. Many voted for me as a personality." A CDU councilor answered: "No, he must represent the interest of the community not those of his party. But there may be some exceptions—in cultural affairs [*Kulturpolitik*], for example. In the retention of religious instruction in the schools."

A second recent survey of municipal officeholders also indicates the prevalence of above-party attitudes among party-affiliated councilmen. Respondents declared they were free of party connections in *Gemeinde* matters and underlined the inappropriateness of party politics to courthouse politics.[15] The idea that partisan struggles should not disrupt communal harmony is reinforced by the belief that the function of the local council is to represent the city as an historical and social entity against the outside world.[16]

The tie-in with the national party system, however weak, is a handicap in the entrenchment of local parties. Although a local partisan candidate or councilor may not appeal to local voters on a strictly partisan platform, he has still adopted a party label. And parties are widely identified as representing groups intruding upon the common good of the community. On the other hand, local voter group representatives by definition indicate that their main orientation is toward communal concerns. Parties are suspected of being

15. Luckmann, p. 190.
16. Ibid., pp. 138–42.

transformers of functional cleavages into political issues where territorial cleavages are equally important. Local parties are deprived of their functional social bases of support and usurped by local voter groups in territorial support bases.

A multitude of factors thus combine to keep political parties out of local elections entirely or to ensure their electoral weakness. Many communes lack the social bases supportive of partisan conflict. The parties themselves may not push local expansion—either because of its marginal value to the national vote or because of their lack of staying power in the local elections which they have penetrated. This lack of local entrenchment may in turn be related to party inability to translate political cleavages into political resources.

8. The Relationship of Parties to Local Electoral Behavior

As a number of studies of local politics have shown, voter alignment varies tremendously within nations. The structured contexts of electoral behavior exert a tremendous influence on the patterns of that behavior. Previous research on Germany, as with much other comparative research, has been confined to the national aggregation of electoral data. In this study, we have investigated the behavior of local voters to discern relationships between local and national electorates and to delineate the role of political parties in structuring the vote. The data bases were the municipalities in Rhineland-Palatinate for the first two decades of the Federal Republic.

The examination indicates that two electoral games are played—national and local. Voting behavior in a community in national elections is largely unrelated to voting behavior in that same community in local elections.[1] The major difference derives from strong local resistance to partisan politics.

A tradition of personal relationships between local notables and their clients ensures that a formal political process (voting) merely reinforces informal positions. Approximately 50 per cent of the *Gemeinden* avoid any form of electoral competition, through plurality elections. Almost two-fifths of municipal officeholders thus achieve power uncontested.

Elements of a traditional relationship between leaders and followers persist even in communes with competitive list elections. Groups organized around local notables may compete quite actively among themselves, but partisan alignment is not a political resource in these local games. The electoral superiority of local voter groups has not been overcome by local branches of national parties: three-

---

1. For a discussion of this phenomenon in France, see Mark Kesselman, "Overinstitutionalization and Political Constraint," p. 37.

fourths of local elections occur without the presence of partisan lists. The breakdown of systems of local rule, where it is happening at all, is an infinitely slow process. But political parties contested more local elections in 1948 than in 1969, and the tendency to switch to lower levels of politicization in successive elections is more characteristic of most *Gemeinden* than is movement toward more politicized contests.

The inability of a party system to develop strong roots at the local level has socioeconomic, cultural, and political factors. Many municipalities lack the economic diversity which sustains partisan competition. Economic growth of itself is not a sufficient condition for partisan mobilization; rather, specific constellations of socioeconomic development are required. Urbanization, with its two components of growth toward larger units and a tertiary economy, is most supportive of local partisan mobilization. De facto, most *Gemeinden* do not possess such characteristics. The economic factor alone, however, cannot adequately explain variations in the politicization of local elections. Norwegian communes at roughly the same stage of economic development are politicized to a greater degree than are the German communes. The German culture is a decisive factor. The penchant for avoiding conflict and the distrust of political parties are widespread throughout German society. To be "above parties" and partisan conflict becomes more desirable at the local level because of the more general aspects of a communal culture.

German *Gemeinden*, like Swiss communes, have a long history of independence which their members cherish. In Germany, as in France,[2] opposition to political parties is one method of maintaining communal autonomy and resisting the encroachment of national governmental power. In this "climate of opinion," candidates for local office must vow their independence and desire to work for an unpartisan community good. The social bases of German politics are, thus, dominated by communal interests. Voter alignment is determined according to local cleavages rather than cross-local cleavages. That national and state electoral loyalties do not appear at the local level with much intensity is revealed by a consideration of determinants of CDU and SPD vote at the various electoral levels. Religion and social class account for far more national and state party-vote

2. Ibid., pp. 21–44.

relationships than local. The extent of the separation is clearly apparent in the CDU local electoral position. Although supported by a CDU state government and favorable demographic population characteristics, it achieves a mere one-fourth of the vote in local elections in Rhineland-Palatinate.

The national party system itself is a contributor to the scarcity of local political parties. The dispersion of state and national party votes shows little relation to local electoral efforts. To a party seeking state and national power, local entry offers few incentives.

Local voters go to the poll in high numbers, largely without the stimulus of political parties (indeed, partisan competition shows some signs of depressing the turnout in local contests). Turnout in local elections equals turnout in national elections and far surpasses turnout in state elections. The same attributes of *Gemeinde* life, such as smallness of territory and prevalence of face-to-face contacts, which hinder partisan mobilization, encourage high voter participation through social pressures. Party growth is, thus, impossible through increased voter turnout. For change to occur, the perceptions and actions of the voters must first become reoriented.

The presence of local citizens who are highly mobilized but not in a partisan way raised doubts as to the extent that *Gemeinden* politics might be considered residual appendages of an evolving party system. Where such widespread indifference or resistance to parties exists, parties do not fulfill positive integrative functions.[3] The great social, economic, and political change that has occurred in postwar Germany has not been matched by corresponding politicization of local units. A local party system has been neither a necessary nor an efficient linkage between citizens and their government. The transformation of the national party system has occurred without strong partisan roots at the local level.

---

3. See Edinger, *Politics in Germany*, pp. 276–85, for a discussion of the integrative functions of the German party system.

Appendixes

A. THE CONSTITUTION OF RHINELAND-PALATINATE

Article 49

"The *Gemeinden* are exclusively responsible for all local administration within their area. They may assume any public function, insofar as such function is not exclusively assigned by explicit legal provision to other agencies in the vital interests of the public.

"*Gemeindeverbaende* have the same position within the limitations of their legal jurisdiction.

"The right of self-government is guaranteed to the *Gemeinden* and *Gemeindeverbaende*. State supervision is limited to making certain that their administration is exercised in accordance with the laws.

"By law or ordinance state functions may be delegated to *Gemeinden* and *Gemeindeverbaende*, or to their chief officials, for execution, according to instructions.

"Through an equitable distribution of tax revenue, the state must insure to *Gemeinden* and *Gemeindeverbaende* the funds required to exercise their own functions and those delegated to them. For their voluntary public activities the state places sources of income at their disposal which shall be administered on their own responsibility.

"Conflicts involving legal relations between *Gemeinden* and their citizens will be settled by the administrative courts."

Article 50

"In all *Gemeinden* and *Gemeindeverbaende* representative bodies are to be elected by the citizens on the basis of the principles of Article 76. These representative bodies are entitled to elect the principal officials."

Article 76

"All popular votes (elections, initiatives and referenda) on the basis of this Constitution are general, equal, direct, secret and free.

"All citizens are qualified voters who are 21 years old and have resided in the *Land* for half a year unless they have been deprived of their civil legal status or their civic rights." [amended: . . . qualified voters who are 18 years old]

Source: Harold O. Lewis, *New Constitutions in Occupied Germany* (Washington: Foundation for Foreign Affairs, 1948), pp. 117–18, 98.

B. Synopsis of Local Election Laws (September 1960)

State	Electoral System	Petition Requirements[a]	Restrictive Clause[b]
Hesse	PR	10 for parties, twice the number of elected councilors for local voter groups.	5%
Rhineland-Palatinate	PR; if 1 or no lists filed, plurality election.	5 for parties represented in preceding council; otherwise, 2% of eligible voters within the boundaries of 10–200 signatures.	5%
Bavaria	Modified PR; if 1 or no lists filed, plurality election. Direct election of mayor.	10 for parties and local voter groups represented in preceding council; otherwise, 4 times the number of elected councilors.	None
North Rhine–Westphalia	Plurality and PR; minimum of 50% of all seats determined by reserve lists.	5–20 for parties not holding at least 3 Landtag seats and for individual candidates.	For seat distribution by list, 5%.
Baden-Wuerttemberg	See Bavaria	10–250 for parties not represented in Landtag or preceding council and for local voter groups not in preceding council.	None
Schleswig-Holstein	PR and plurality elections	5–20 for parties not represented in Bundestag, Landtag, or preceding council and for individual candidates.	For seat distribution by list, 5%.

B. SYNOPSIS OF LOCAL ELECTION LAWS (SEPTEMBER 1960) (*Cont.*)

State	Electoral System	Petition Requirements[a]	Restrictive Clause[b]
Lower Saxony	Modified **PR**	10–30 for all except parties represented in *Bundestag* or *Landtag*.	None
Saar	PR	3 times the number of elected councilors except for parties represented in *Bundestag* or *Landtag*.	5%

SOURCE: Werner W. Grundmann, *Die Rathausparteien* (Goettingen: Verlag Otto Schwarz & Co., 1960), pp. 110–11.
a. Signatures required for candidacy.
b. Percentage of vote required for representation.

C. ALLOCATION OF COUNCIL SEATS BY SIZE OF *Gemeinde* (1960)

Number of inhabitants	Number of seats
1 to 150	5
150 to 500	7
500 to 1,000	11
1,000 to 3,000	15
3,000 to 10,000	19
10,000 to 20,000	25
20,000 to 40,000	31
40,000 to 60,000	37
60,000 to 80,000	43
80,000 to 100,000	47
100,000 and more	51

D. CORRELATION MATRIX OF SOCIOECONOMIC VARIABLES

	Density	Streets	Size	Tax	Comein	Trade	Services	Whtcol	Femec	Agric	Selfempl	Comaus	Prod
Streets	.61												
Size	.80	.85											
Tax	.45	.32	.38										
Comein	.46	.24	.32	.63									
Trade	.49	.24	.32	.33	.44								
Services	.41	.25	.33	.33	.41	.42							
Whtcol	.67	.40	.51	.48	.60	.78	.64						
Femec	-.33	-.14	-.18	-.23	-.34	-.53	-.22	-.52					
Agric	-.59	-.27	-.38	-.42	-.56	-.67	-.57	-.77	.64				
Selfempl	-.41	-.16	-.25	-.21	-.36	-.39	-.31	-.53	.50	.74			
Comaus	.16	-.15	-.08	-.09	.08	.38	.13	.34	-.60	-.66	-.68		
Product	.41	.15	.22	.28	.39	.32	.08	.42	-.57	-.83	-.72	.70	
Manuals	.35	.09	.16	.20	.33	.35	.24	.40	-.56	-.82	-.77	.77	.89

Density = population density
Streets = municipal streets
Size = population size
Tax = community tax strength
Comein = commuters (*Einpendler*)
Trade = trade
Services = services

Whtcol = white collar workers and civil servants
Femec = female employees
Agric = agriculture
Selfempl = self-employed
Comaus = commuters (*Auspendler*)
Product = production
Manuals = manual workers

E. Relationship of Communal Sociostructural Characteristics to CDU Vote in 1965 National and 1963 State Elections

Demographic Correlates of CDU Vote in National and State Elections

Sociostructural Variables	CDU vote	
	1965	1963
Population density	−.18	−.17
Catholics	.84	.85
Refugees	−.15	−.15
Agriculture	.27	.26
Production	−.22	−.21
Trade	−.18	−.18
White collar workers and civil servants	−.22	−.18
Manual workers	−.20	−.18
Female employees	.26	.25
Self-employed	.21	.20
Auspendler	−.23	−.22
Community tax strength	−.21	−.21

NOTE: The data unit is the *Gemeinde*. The demographic variables stem from the 1961 census. The 1965 party percentages are those of the second ballot. All the Pearson product-moment correlation coefficients are significant at the .001 level.

Multiple Stepwise Regression of CDU Vote in 1965 National and 1963 State Elections

Year	Independent Variable	Multiple R	Variance Accounted For
1965	Catholics	.838	.701
	Refugees	.914	.836
	Trade	.925	.855
1963	Catholics	.848	.719
	Refugees	.922	.851
	Trade	.933	.870

NOTE: The findings are reported only for those variables whose contribution to R^2 was greater than 1 per cent. All correlations are significant at the .001 level.

F. RELATIONSHIP OF COMMUNAL SOCIOSTRUCTURAL CHARACTERISTICS
TO SPD VOTE IN 1965 NATIONAL AND 1963 STATE ELECTIONS

DEMOGRAPHIC CORRELATES OF SPD VOTE IN
NATIONAL AND STATE ELECTIONS

Sociostructural Variables	SPD Vote	
	1965	1963
Population density	.25	.24
Catholics	−.72	−.73
Refugees	.17	.14
Agriculture	**−.43**	−.42
Production	**.38**	.37
Trade	.28	.29
Services	.20	.19
White collar workers and civil servants	.32	.32
Manual workers	.38	.35
Female employees	−.38	−.36
Self-employed	−.38	−.37
Auspendler	.40	.40
Community tax strength	−.20	−.21

NOTE: The data unit is the *Gemeinde*. The demographic variables stem from the 1961 census. The 1965 party percentages are those of the second ballot. All the Pearson product-moment correlation coefficients are significant at the .001 level.

MULTIPLE STEPWISE REGRESSION OF SPD VOTE IN
1965 NATIONAL AND 1963 STATE ELECTIONS

Year	Independent Variable	Multiple R	Variance Accounted For
1965	Catholics	.718	.515
	Refugees	.780	.639
	Agriculture	.854	.730
	Auspendler	.862	.742
1963	Catholics	.734	.540
	Agriculture	.809	.655
	Refugees	.856	.732

NOTE: The findings are reported only for those variables whose individual contribution to R^2 was greater than 1 per cent. All correlations are significant at the .001 level.

Bibliography

BOOKS

Adrian, Charles R., and Press, Charles. *Governing Urban America.* 4th ed. New York: McGraw-Hill Book Company, 1972.

Almond, Gabriel, and Verba, Sidney. *The Civic Culture.* Boston: Little, Brown and Company, 1965.

Beer, Ruediger Robert. *Die Gemeinde.* Munich: Guenter Olzog Verlag, 1970.

Behn, Hans Ulrich. *Die Bundesrepublik Deutschland.* Munich: Guenter Olzog Verlag, 1974.

Berelson, Bernard R.; Lazarsfeld, Paul F.; and McPhee, William N. *Voting.* Chicago: The University of Chicago Press, 1954.

Campbell, Angus; Converse, Philip E.; Miller, Warren E.; and Stokes, Donald E. *The American Voter: An Abridgement.* New York: John Wiley & Sons, Inc., 1964.

Codding, George, Jr. *Governing the Commune of Veyrier: Politics in Swiss Local Government.* Boulder: Bureau of Governmental Research of the University of Colorado, 1967.

Conradt, David P. *The West German Party System: An Ecological Analysis of Social Structure and Voting Behavior, 1961–1969.* Beverly Hills: Sage Publications, Inc., 1972.

Dahl, Robert A., ed. *Political Opposition in Western Democracies.* New Haven: Yale University Press, 1966.

Dahrendorf, Ralf. *Society and Democracy in Germany.* New York: Doubleday and Company, Inc., 1967.

Dogan, Mattei, and Rokkan, Stein, eds. *Quantitative Ecological Analyses in the Social Sciences.* Cambridge: The MIT Press, 1969.

Edinger, Lewis J. *Politics in Germany.* Boston: Little, Brown and Company, 1968.

Ellwein, Thomas. *Das Regierungssystem der Bundesrepublik Deutschland.* Cologne: Westdeutscher Verlag, 1965.

Epstein, Leon. *Political Parties in Western Democracies.* New York: Frederick A. Praeger, Inc., 1967.

Faul, Erwin. *Wahlen und Waehler in Westdeutschland.* Villingen / Schwarzwald: Ring-Verlag, 1960.

Gemmecke, Vera. *Parteien im Wahlkampf.* Meisenheim am Glan: Verlag Anton Hain, 1967.

Greenstein, Fred I. *The American Party System and the American People.* 2d ed. Englewood Cliffs: Prentice-Hall, Inc., 1970.

Grundmann, Werner. *Die Rathausparteien.* Goettingen: Verlag Otto Schwarz & Co., 1960.

Harris, G. Montagu. *Comparative Local Government.* London: William Brendon & Sons, Ltd., 1948.

Hawley, Willis D. *Nonpartisan Elections and the Case for Party Politics.* New York: John Wiley & Sons, 1973.

Heidenheimer, Arnold J. *Adenauer and the CDU.* The Hague: Martinus Nijhoff, 1960.

————. *The Governments of Germany.* 3d ed. New York: Thomas Y. Crowell Co., 1971.

Hirsch-Weber, Wolfgang, and Schuetz, Klaus. *Waehler und Gewaehlte.* Berlin: Verlag Franz Vahlen GmbH, 1957.

Hiscocks, Richard. *Democracy in Western Germany.* London: Oxford University Press, 1957.

Holt, Stephen. *Six European States.* London: Hamish Hamilton Ltd., 1970.

Huntington, Samuel P. *Political Order in Changing Societies.* New Haven: Yale University Press, 1968.

Jacob, Herbert. *German Administration since Bismarck: Central Authority versus Local Autonomy.* New Haven: Yale University Press, 1963.

Jaeggi, Urs. *Berggemeinden im Wandel.* Bern: Verlag Paul Haupt, 1965.

Kaack, Heino. *Geschichte und Struktur des deutschen Parteiensystems.* Opladen: Westdeutscher Verlag, 1971.

————. *Wer kommt in den Bundestag?* Opladen: C. W. Leske Verlag, 1969.

Kesselman, Mark. *The Ambiguous Consensus: A Study of Local Government in France.* New York: Alfred A. Knopf, Inc., 1967.

Key, V. O., Jr. *Politics, Parties, and Pressure Groups.* 2d ed. New York: Thomas Y. Crowell Co., 1948.

————. *Southern Politics.* New York: Vintage Books, 1949.

Kitzinger, Uwe W. *German Electoral Politics.* Oxford: Oxford University Press, 1960.

Koetter, Herbert. *Struktur und Funktion von Landgemeinden im Einflussbereich einer deutschen Mittelstadt.* Darmstadt: Eduard Roether Verlag, 1952.

Koettgen, Arnold. *Die Gemeinde und der Bundesgesetzgeber.* Stuttgart: Verlag W. Kohlhammer GmbH, 1957.

LaPalombara, Joseph, and Weiner, Myron, eds. *Political Parties and Political Development.* Princeton: Princeton University Press, 1966.

Lewis, Harold O. *New Constitutions in Occupied Germany.* Washington, D.C.: Foundation for Foreign Affairs, 1948.

Lipset, Seymour M., and Rokkan, Stein, eds. *Party Systems and Voter Alignments: Cross-National Perspectives.* New York: The Free Press, 1967.

Litchfield, Edward H., and Associates. *Governing Postwar Germany.* Ithaca: Cornell University Press, 1953.

Luckmann, Benita. *Politik in einer deutschen Kleinstadt.* Stuttgart: Ferdinand Enke Verlag, 1970.

Mayntz, Renate. *Soziale Schichtung und Sozialer Wandel in einer Industriegemeinde.* Stuttgart: Ferdinand Enke Verlag, 1958.

Merritt, Richard L., and Rokkan, Stein, eds. *Comparing Nations: The Use of Quantitative Data in Cross-National Research.* New Haven: Yale University Press, 1966.

Milbrath, Lester. *Political Participation.* Chicago: Rand McNally & Co., 1965.

Oel, Peter. *Die Gemeinde im Blickfeld ihrer Buerger.* Stuttgart: Verlag W. Kohlhammer, 1972.

Pappi, Franz Urban. *Wahlverhalten und Politische Kultur.* Meisenheim am Glan: Verlag Anton Hain, 1970.

Peters, Hans, ed. *Handbuch der kommunalen Wissenschaft und Praxis*, vol. 1, *Kommunalverfassung*; vol. 2, *Kommunale Verwaltung*. Berlin: Springer-Verlag, 1956, 1957.

Pfizer, Theodor. *Kommunalpolitik*. Stuttgart: Verlag W. Kohlhammer, 1973.

Rokkan, Stein, ed. *Approaches to the Study of Political Participation*. Bergen: Christian Michelsen Institute, 1962.

Rokkan, Stein; Campbell, Angus; Torsvik, Per; and Valen, Henry, eds. *Citizens, Elections, Parties*. New York: David McKay Company, Inc., 1970.

Rokkan, Stein, and Meyriat, Jean, eds. *International Guide to Electoral Statistics*, vol. 1, *National Elections in Western Europe*. The Hague: Mouton, 1969.

Roth, Werner. *Dorf im Wandel*. Frankfurt am Main: Verlag Hugo Hassmueller, 1968.

Ruediger, Vera. *Die kommunalen Wahlvereinigungen in Hessen*. Meisenheim am Glan: Verlag Anton Hain, 1966.

Scheuch, Erwin K., and Wildenmann, Rudolf. *Zur Soziologie der Wahl*. Opladen: Westdeutscher Verlag, 1965.

Schwonke, Martin, and Herlyn, Ulfert. *Wolfsburg: Soziologische Analyse einer jungen Industriestadt*. Stuttgart: Ferdinand Enke Verlag, 1967.

Smith, T. Lynn, and Zopf, Paul E., Jr. *Principles of Inductive Rural Sociology*. Philadelphia: F. A. Davis Co., 1970.

Sorauf, Frank J. *Party Politics in America*. 2d ed. Boston: Little, Brown and Co., 1972.

Tarrow, Sidney. *Peasant Communism in Southern Italy*. New Haven: Yale University Press, 1967.

Utzinger, Ernst. *Die freie politische Gemeinde in der Schweiz und im Ausland*. Zurich: Scientia-Verlag, 1946.

Warren, Roland L. *The Community in America*. 2d ed. New York: Rand McNally & Company, 1973.

Wells, Roger H. *The States in West German Federalism*. New York: Bookman Associates, 1961.

Wurzbacher, Gerhard, and Pflaum, Renate, eds. *Das Dorf im Spannungsfeld industrieller Entwicklung*. Stuttgart: Ferdinand Enke Verlag, 1954.

Ziebill, Otto. *Politische Parteien und kommunale Selbstverwaltung*. Stuttgart: Verlag W. Kohlhammer, 1972.

ARTICLES AND UNPUBLISHED MATERIAL

Adrian, Charles R. "Some Characteristics of Nonpartisan Elections." In *Democracy in Urban America*, edited by Oliver P. Williams and Charles Press. Chicago: Rand McNally & Co., 1961.

Alford, Robert R., and Lee, Eugene C. "Voting Turnout in American Cities." *The American Political Science Review* 67, no. 3 (September 1968): 796–813.

Allardt, Erik. "Implications of Within-Nation Variations and Regional Imbalances for Cross-National Research." In *Comparing Nations: The Use of Quantitative Data in Cross-National Research*, edited by Richard L. Merritt and Stein Rokkan. New Haven: Yale University Press, 1966.

Barnes, Samuel H.; Grace, Frank; Pollock, James K.; and Sperlich, Peter W. "The German Party System and the 1961 Federal Election." *The American Political Science Review* 56, no. 4 (December 1962): 899–914.

Becker, Erich. "Entwicklung der deutschen Gemeinden und Gemeindeverbaende im Hinblick auf die Gegenwart." In *Handbuch der kommunalen Wissenschaft und Praxis*, vol. 1, *Kommunalverfassung*, edited by Hans Peters. Berlin: Springer-Verlag, 1956.

Beckers, Hans-Joachim. "Die kommunale Machstruktur in einer Pendlergemeinde." Ph.D. dissertation, University of Cologne, 1968.

Campbell, Angus. "The Political Implications of Community Identification." In *Approaches to the Study of Politics*, edited by Roland Young. Evanston: Northwestern University Press, 1958.

Conradt, David P. "Electoral Law Politics in West Germany." *Political Studies* 18, no. 3 (September 1970): 341–56.

———. "West Germany: A Remade Political Culture?" *Comparative Political Studies* 7, no. 2 (July 1974): 222–38.

Cutright, Phillips. "Nonpartisan Electoral Systems in American Cities." In *Democracy in Urban America*, edited by Oliver P. Williams and Charles Press. 2d ed. Chicago: Rand McNally & Co., 1970.

Dahrendorf, Ralf. "The New Germanies: Restoration, Revolution, Reconstruction." In *Politics in Europe*, edited by Arend Lijphart. Englewood Cliffs: Prentice-Hall, Inc., 1969.

Dewey, Richard. "The Rural-Urban Continuum: Real but Relatively Unimportant." *The American Journal of Sociology* 67, no. 1 (July 1960): 60–66.

Edinger, Lewis J. "Political Change in Germany." *Comparative Politics* 2, no. 4 (July 1970): 549–78.

Frye, Charles E. "Parties and Pressure Groups in Weimar and Bonn." In *Politics in Europe*, edited by Arend Lijphart. Englewood Cliffs: Prentice-Hall, Inc., 1969.

Gunlicks, Arthur B. "Intraparty Democracy in Western Germany." *Comparative Politics* 2, no. 2 (January 1970): 229–49.

———. "Representative and Party at the Local Level in Western Germany: The Case of Lower Saxony." Ph.D. dissertation, Georgetown University, 1967.

———. "Representative Role Perceptions among Local Councilors in Western Germany." *The Journal of Politics* 31, no. 2 (May 1969): 443–64.

Hamilton, Howard D. "The Municipal Voter: Voting and Non-voting in City Elections." *The American Political Science Review* 65, no. 4 (December 1971): 1135–40.

Hartenstein, Wolfgang, and Liepelt, Klaus. "Party Members and Party Voters in West Germany." *Acta Sociologica* 6, nos. 1–2 (1962): 43–52.

Heberle, Rudolph. "Analysis of a Neo-Fascist Party: The NPD." *Polity* 3, no. 1 (Fall 1970): 126–34.

Kaase, Max. "Determinants of Voting Behavior in the West German General Election of 1969." Manuscript. Mannheim: Institut fuer Sozialwissenschaften, 1969.

Kaltefleiter, Werner. "The Impact of the Election of 1969 and the Formation of the New Government on the German Party System." *Comparative Politics* 2, no. 4 (July 1970): 593–603.

Kesselman, Mark. "Overinstitutionalization and Political Constraint." *Comparative Politics* 3, no. 1 (October 1970): 21–44.

King, Anthony. "Political Parties in Western Democracies: Some Sceptical Reflections." *Polity* 2, no. 2 (Winter 1969): 111–41.

Klingemann, Hans D., and Pappi, Franz Urban. "The 1969 Bundestag Election in the Federal Republic of Germany." *Comparative Politics* 2, no. 4 (July 1970): 523–48.

Koenig, René. "Die Gemeinde im Blickfeld der Soziologie." In *Handbuch der kommunalen Wissenschaft und Praxis*, vol. 1, *Kommunalverfassung*, edited by Hans Peters. Berlin: Springer-Verlag, 1956.

Koettgen, Arnold. "Wesen und Rechtsform der Gemeinden und Gemeindeverbaende." In *Handbuch der kommunalen Wissenschaft und Praxis*, vol. 1, *Kommunalverfassung*, edited by Hans Peters. Berlin: Springer-Verlag, 1956.

Landers, Linda J. "The Decline in the Authority and Prestige of Ludwig Erhard as West German Chancellor." Master's thesis, University of Florida, 1969.

LaPalombara, Joseph, and Weiner, Myron. "The Origin and Development of Political Parties." In *Political Parties and Political Development*, edited by Joseph LaPalombara and Myron Weiner. Princeton: Princeton University Press, 1966.

Laumann, Edward O., and Pappi, Franz Urban. "New Directions in the Study of Community Elites." *American Sociological Review* 38 (April 1973): 212–30.

Lemarchand, Rene, and Legg, Keith. "Political Clientelism and Development." *Comparative Politics* 4, no. 4 (January 1972): 149–78.

Linz, Juan. "Cleavage and Consensus in West German Politics: The Early Fifties." In *Party Systems and Voter Alignments: Cross-National Perspectives*, edited by Seymour M. Lipset and Stein Rokkan. New York: The Free Press, 1967.

Lipset, Seymour M., and Rokkan, Stein. "Cleavage Structures, Party Systems, and Voter Alignments: An Introduction." In *Party Systems and Voter Alignments: Cross-National Perspectives*, edited by Seymour M. Lipset and Stein Rokkan. New York: The Free Press, 1967.

Loewenberg, Gerhard. "The Remaking of the German Party System: Political and Socio-economic Factors." *Polity* 1, no. 1 (Fall 1968): 87–113.

Lowi, Theodore. "Toward Functionalism in Political Science: The Case of Innovation in Party Systems." *The American Political Science Review* 57, no. 3 (September 1963): 570–83.

Merkl, Peter H. "Political Cleavages and Party Systems" (review article). *World Politics* 21, no. 3 (April 1969): 469–85.

Pappi, Franz Urban. "Sozialstruktur und soziale Schichtung in einer Kleinstadt mit heterogener Bevoelkerung." *Koelner Zeitschrift fuer Soziologie und Sozialpsychologie* 25 (1973): 23–74.

Pappi, Franz Urban, and Laumann, Edward O. "Gesellschaftliche Wertorientierungen und politisches Verhalten." *Zietschrift fuer Soziologie* 3, no. 2 (April 1974): 157–88.

Pflaum, Renate. "Politische Fuehrung und politische Beteiligung als Ausdruck gemeindlicher Selbstgestaltung." In *Das Dorf im Spannungsfeld industrieller Entwicklung*, edited by Gerhard Wurzbacher and Renate Pflaum. Stuttgart: Ferdinand Enke Verlag, 1954.

Putnam, Robert D. "Political Attitudes and the Local Community." *The American Political Science Review* 60, no. 3 (September 1966): 640–54.

Ranney, Austin. "The Utility and Limitations of Aggregate Data in the Study of Electoral Behavior." In *Essays on the Behavioral Study of Politics*, edited by Austin Ranney. Urbana: University of Illinois Press, 1962.

Rokkan, Stein. "Citizen Participation in Political Life: A Comparison of Data for Norway and the United States of America." In *Citizens, Elections,*

Parties, edited by Stein Rokkan, Angus Campbell, Per Torsvik, and Henry Valen. New York: David McKay Company, Inc., 1970.

―――. "Electoral Mobilization, Party Competition, and National Integration." In *Political Parties and Political Development*, edited by Joseph LaPalombara and Myron Weiner. Princeton: Princeton University Press, 1966.

―――. "Methods and Models in the Comparative Study of Nation-Building." In *Citizens, Elections, Parties*, edited by Stein Rokkan, Angus Campbell, Per Torsvik, and Henry Valen. New York: David McKay Company, Inc., 1970.

Rokkan, Stein, and Valen, Henry. "The Mobilization of the Periphery: Data on Turnout, Party Membership and Candidate Recruitment in Norway." In *Citizens, Elections, Parties*, edited by Stein Rokkan, Angus Campbell, Per Torsvik, and Henry Valen. New York: David McKay Company, Inc., 1970.

Rokkan, Stein, and Valen, Henry. "Regional Contrasts in Norwegian Politics." In *Mass Politics: Studies in Political Sociology*, edited by Erik Allardt and Stein Rokkan. New York: The Free Press, 1970.

Sartori, Giovanni. "From the Sociology of Politics to Political Sociology." In *Politics and the Social Sciences*, edited by Seymour M. Lipset. New York: Oxford University Press, 1969.

Scarrow, Howard A. "The Function of Political Parties: A Critique of the Literature and the Approach." *Journal of Politics* 24, no. 4 (November 1967): 770–90.

Scheuch, Erwin K. "Cross-National Comparisons Using Aggregate Data: Some Substantive and Methodological Problems." In *Comparing Nations: The Use of Quantitative Data in Cross-National Research*, edited by Richard L. Merritt and Stein Rokkan. New Haven: Yale University Press, 1966.

―――. "Social Context and Individual Behavior." In *Quantitative Ecological Analyses in the Social Sciences*, edited by Mattei Dogan and Stein Rokkan. Cambridge: The MIT Press, 1969.

Segal, David R., and Meyer, Marshall W. "The Social Context of Political Participation." In *Quantitative Ecological Analyses in the Social Sciences*, edited by Mattei Dogan and Stein Rokkan. Cambridge: The MIT Press, 1969.

Stiefbold, Rodney. "The Significance of Void Ballots in West German Elections." *The American Political Science Review* 59, no. 2 (June 1965): 391–407.

Tarrow, Sidney. "The Urban-Rural Cleavage in Political Involvement: The Case of France." *The American Political Science Review* 65, no. 2 (June 1971): 341–57.

Valen, Henry. "Norway: The 1967 Local Elections." In *Scandinavian Political Studies*, vol. 3, *1968*, edited by Per Torsvik. New York: Columbia University Press, 1969.

Valen, Henry, and Katz, Daniel. "An Electoral Contest in a Norwegian Province." In *Community Political Systems*, edited by Morris Janowitz. Glencoe: The Free Press, 1961.

Verba, Sidney. "Germany: The Remaking of a Political Culture." In *Political Culture and Political Development*, edited by Lucien Pye and Sidney Verba. Princeton: Princeton University Press, 1969.

Warnecke, Steven. "The Future of Rightist Extremism in West Germany." *Comparative Politics* 2, no. 4 (July 1970): 629–52.

109

GOVERNMENT PUBLICATIONS

Bavaria. *Beitraege zur Statistik Bayerns, Heft* 220, *Kommunalwahlen in Bayern am 27. Maerz 1960.* Munich: Statistisches Landesamt, 1961.
Germany. *Statistisches Bundesamt. Amtliches Gemeindeverzeichnis fuer die Bundesrepublik Deutschland.* Stuttgart: W. Kohlhammer GmbH, 1963.
———. Federal Statistical Office. *Handbook of Statistics for the Federal Republic of Germany.* Stuttgart: W. Kohlhammer GmbH, 1970.
———. *Statistisches Bundesamt. Statistisches Jahrbuch fuer die Bundesrepublik Deutschland, 1968, 1970, 1972, 1973.* Stuttgart: W. Kohlhammer GmbH, 1968, 1970, 1972, 1973.
Hesse. *Beitraege zur Statistik Hessens.* Nr. 54, *Die Kommunalwahlen am 22. Oktober 1972.* Wiesbaden: Statistisches Landesamt, 1973.
Lower Saxony. *Statistik von Niedersachsen, Band 118, Die Kommunalwahlen in Niedersachsen am 29. September 1968.* Part 1. Hanover: Landesverwaltungsamt, 1969.
Rhineland-Palatinate. *Statistik von Rheinland-Pfalz, Band 24, Die Kommunalwahlen am 9. November 1952 in Rheinland-Pfalz.* Bad Ems: Statistisches Landesamt, 1953.
———. *Statistik von Rheinland-Pfalz, Band 39. Die Wahlen zum Landtag und Bundestag in Rheinland-Pfalz 1947–1955, Ergebnisse in den Gemeinden.* Bad Ems: Statistisches Landesamt, 1956.
———. *Statistik von Rheinland-Pfalz, Band 46, Die Kommunalwahlen am 11. November 1956 in Rheinland-Pfalz.* Bad Ems: Statistisches Landesamt, 1957.
———. *Statistik von Rheinland-Pfalz, Band 53, Die Wahl zum Dritten Bundestag in Rheinland-Pfalz am 15. September 1957.* Bad Ems: Statistisches Landesamt, 1958.
———. *Statistik von Rheinland-Pfalz, Band 69, Die Wahl zum Landtag in Rheinland-Pfalz am 19. April 1959.* Bad Ems: Statistisches Landesamt, 1959.
———. *Statistik von Rheinland-Pfalz, Band 87, Die Kommunalwahlen in Rheinland-Pfalz am 23. Oktober 1960.* Bad Ems: Statistisches Landesamt, 1961.
———. *Statistik von Rheinland-Pfalz, Band 94, Die Wahl zum Vierten Bundestag in Rheinland-Pfalz am 17. September 1961.* Bad Ems: Statistisches Landesamt, 1961.
———. *Statistik von Rheinland-Pfalz, Band 109, Gemeindestatistik Rheinland-Pfalz 1960/61, Teil* I: *Bevoelkerung und Erwerbstaetigkeit.* Bad Ems: Statistisches Landesamt, 1964.
———. *Statistik von Rheinland-Pfalz, Band 110, Gemeindestatistik Rheinland-Pfalz 1960/61, Teil* II: *Gebaeude und Wohnungen, Teil* III: *Arbeitsstaetten (ohne Landwirtschaft).* Bad Ems: Statistisches Landesamt, 1963.
———. *Statistik von Rheinland-Pfalz, Band 111, Gemeindestatistik Rheinland-Pfalz 1960/61, Teil* IV: *Betriebsstruktur der Landwirtschaft, Teil* V: *Gemeindefinanzen.* Bad Ems: Statistisches Landesamt, 1962.
———. *Statistik von Rheinland-Pfalz, Band 130, Die Wahl zum Landtag in Rheinland-Pfalz am 31. Maerz 1963.* Bad Ems: Statistisches Landesamt, 1963.
———. *Statistik von Rheinland-Pfalz, Band 142, Die Kommunalwahlen in Rheinland-Pfalz am 25. Oktober 1964.* Bad Ems: Statistisches Landesamt, 1965.
———. *Statistik von Rheinland-Pfalz, Band 152, Die Wahl zum Fuenften*

Deutschen Bundestag in Rheinland-Pfalz am 19. September 1969. Bad Ems: Statistisches Landesamt, 1966.

————. *Statistik von Rheinland-Pfalz, Band 171, Die Wahl zum Landtag in Rheinland-Pfalz am 23. April 1967.* Bad Ems: Statistisches Landesamt, 1967.

————. *Statistik von Rheinland-Pfalz, Band 195, Die Kommunalwahlen in Rheinland-Pfalz am 8. Juni 1969.* Bad Ems: Statistisches Landesamt, 1969.

————. *Statistik von Rheinland-Pfalz, Band 203, Die Wahl zum Sechsten Deutschen Bundestag in Rheinland-Pfalz am 28. September 1969.* Bad Ems: Statistisches Landesamt, 1970.

————. *Statistik von Rheinland-Pfalz, Band 245, Die Wahl zum 7. Landtag in Rheinland-Pfalz am 21. Maerz 1971.* Bad Ems: Statistisches Landesamt, 1971.

U.S. Department of State. *The Bonn Constitution: Basic Law for the Federal Republic of Germany.* Washington, D.C.: Government Printing Office, 1949.

UNIVERSITY OF FLORIDA MONOGRAPHS

Social Sciences

1. *The Whigs of Florida, 1845–1854,* by Herbert J. Doherty, Jr.
2. *Austrian Catholics and the Social Question, 1918–1933,* by Alfred Diamant
3. *The Seige of St. Augustine in 1702,* by Charles W. Arnade
4. *New Light on Early and Medieval Japanese Historiography,* by John A. Harrison
5. *The Swiss Press and Foreign Affairs in World War II,* by Frederick H. Hartmann
6. *The American Militia: Decade of Decision, 1789–1800,* by John K. Mahon
7. *The Foundation of Jacques Maritain's Political Philosophy,* by Hwa Yol Jung
8. *Latin American Population Studies,* by T. Lynn Smith
9. *Jacksonian Democracy on the Florida Frontier,* by Arthur W. Thompson
10. *Holman Versus Hughes: Extension of Australian Commonwealth Powers,* by Conrad Joyner
11. *Welfare Economics and Subsidy Programs,* by Milton Z. Kafoglis
12. *Tribune of the Slavophiles: Konstantin Aksakov,* by Edward Chmielewski
13. *City Managers in Politics: An Analysis of Manager Tenure and Termination,* by Gladys M. Kammerer, Charles D. Farris, John M. DeGrove, and Alfred B. Clubok
14. *Recent Southern Economic Development as Revealed by the Changing Structure of Employment,* by Edgar S. Dunn, Jr.
15. *Sea Power and Chilean Independence,* by Donald E. Worcester
16. *The Sherman Antitrust Act and Foreign Trade,* by Andre Simmons
17. *The Origins of Hamilton's Fiscal Policies,* by Donald F. Swanson
18. *Criminal Asylum in Anglo-Saxon Law,* by Charles H. Riggs, Jr.
19. *Colonia Barón Hirsch, A Jewish Agricultural Colony in Argentina,* by Morton D. Winsberg
20. *Time Deposits in Present-Day Commercial Banking,* by Lawrence L. Crum
21. *The Eastern Greenland Case in Historical Perspective,* by Oscar Svarlien
22. *Jacksonian Democracy and the Historians,* by Alfred A. Cave
23. *The Rise of the American Chemistry Profession, 1850–1900,* by Edward H. Beardsley
24. *Aymara Communities and the Bolivian Agrarian Reform,* by William E. Carter
25. *Conservatives in the Progressive Era: The Taft Republicans of 1912,* by Norman M. Wilensky
26. *The Anglo-Norwegian Fisheries Case of 1951 and the Changing Law of the Territorial Sea,* by Teruo Kobayashi
27. *The Liquidity Structure of Firms and Monetary Economics,* by William J. Frazer, Jr.
28. *Russo-Persian Commercial Relations, 1828–1914,* by Marvin L. Entner
29. *The Imperial Policy of Sir Robert Borden,* by Harold A. Wilson
30. *The Association of Income and Educational Achievement,* by Roy L. Lassiter, Jr.
31. *Relation of the People to the Land in Southern Iraq,* by Fuad Baali

32. *The Price Theory of Value in Public Finance*, by Donald R. Escarraz

33. *The Process of Rural Development in Latin America*, by T. Lynn Smith

34. *To Be or Not to Be . . . Existential-Psychological Perspectives on the Self*, edited by Sidney M. Jourard

35. *Politics in a Mexican Community*, by Lawrence S. Graham

36. *A Two-Sector Model of Economic Growth with Technological Progress*, by Frederick Owen Goddard

37. *Florida Studies in the Helping Professions*, by Arthur W. Combs

38. *The Ancient Synagogues of the Iberian Peninsula*, by Don A. Halperin

39. *An Estimate of Personal Wealth in Oklahoma in 1960*, by Richard Edward French

40. *Congressional Oversight of Executive Agencies*, by Thomas A. Henderson

41. *Historians and Meiji Statesmen*, by Richard T. Chang

42. *Welfare Economics and Peak Load Pricing: A Theoretical Application to Municipal Water Utility Practices*, by Robert Lee Greene

43. *Factor Analysis in International Relations: Interpretation, Problem Areas, and an Application*, by Jack E. Vincent

44. *The Sorcerer's Apprentice: The French Scientist's Image of German Science, 1840–1919*, by Harry W. Paul

45. *Community Power Structure: Propositional Inventory, Tests, and Theory*, by Claire W. Gilbert

46. *Human Capital, Technology, and the Role of the United States in International Trade*, by John F. Morrall III

47. *The Segregation Factor in the Florida Democratic Gubernatorial Primary of 1956*, by Helen L. Jacobstein

48. *The Navy Department in the War of 1812*, by Edward K. Eckert

49. *Social Change and the Electoral Process*, by William L. Shade

50. *East from the Andes: Pioneer Settlements in the South American Heartland*, by Raymond E. Crist and Charles M. Nissly

51. *A General Equilibrium Study of the Monetary Mechanism*, by David L. Schulze

52. *The Impact of Trade Destruction on National Incomes: A Study of Europe 1924–1938*, by Philip Friedman

53. *Administration of Justice in Drunk Driving Cases*, by Joseph W. Little

54. *Geographical Aspects of Agricultural Changes in the Ryuku Islands*, by Shannon McCune

55. *Democracy and the Case for Amnesty*, by Alfonso J. Damico

56. *Electoral Politics at the Local Level in the German Federal Republic*, by Linda L. Dolive